a place to close my eyes

Rachel Shelton

To Kasey, Nathaniel, and Samuel:
Who showed me how to love unconditionally and to
Randy who showed me how to love like 1 Corinthians 13:4-5.
Love is patient, love is kind, it does not envy, it does not boast, it is not
proud.
It does not dishonor others, it is not self-seeking, it is not easily angered, it
keeps no record of wrongs.

Prayer of Introduction

My Jesus, every day I give you praise for loving me. You showed me throughout this 2 ½ year journey that You can take the impossible and make it possible. You have guided me through the storms, the trials, the doubt, and the fear. You have taught me to lean on You, and not my own understanding. You have restored more to me than I could ever imagine. I am reminded of the scripture in Ephesians 3:20---
"Now to Him who is able to carry out His purpose and do superabundantly more than all that we dare ask or think, infinitely beyond our greatest prayers, hopes, or dreams, according to His power that is at work within us"
Thank You, Jesus.

The hospital is quiet this time of night. I lean my head against the window, as I look at Momma lying in the sterile bed, and my mind begins to drift to the deep south where I hear the dialect clearly from my past..........................

one

"Anna Marie!" I could hear Momma callin' me. I left the house first thing in the mornin' and wouldn't come home until I could hear that frustration in her voice. Usually at supper time was when she realized I was not there. No one ever noticed.

"Yous better go on home now, Little Anna," said Joes. I looked at him; he was so black. Only white on him was his eyes. Joes lived on the back side of my grandparent's farm in a shack. I reckon he has always lived there. I came to see him near every day. He got real nervous though. He says to me, "Now, Little Anna, what'ch yous doin' here? Yous know yous not supposed to be back here."

I just shrugged my shoulders and said, "no one cares joes. no one even goin' to notice and yous know that to be true." But I picked myself up from the stairs where I had been most of the day listenin' to Joes tell his stories. They was good stories too. I reckon I kept Joes company about as much as he kept me company.

As soon as I got to Joes' place, he always had a cold cup of sweet ice tea for me. One day I say, "joes, how is your tea cold? seein' how yous don't have a frigerator?" Joes grinned and said it was a secret. But one day I saw him bring it up out of the well where he drew his water from. I never told him I knew his secret.

The tea was always in a battered tin cup. It had dents on the sides, almost like it had been hit with somethin'. I reckon Joes didn't have no glass cups, like the ones my Grammy used. The blue and white ones. But I didn't mind. I know Joes, he done and made that ice tea just for me. He seemed to know how thirsty I would be after runnin' from my Grammy's house to his. I would see him standin' on the front porch when I turned the last curve in the road, just before the pond on the right, next to the big crepe myrtle. It's like he just knew when I would be comin' up the long sandy road lined with the pine trees. He always smiled when he seen me runnin' and swattin' away at the gnats, as I ran through the swarm of them. I never understood why those gnats wanted to linger in one place and right at where my head would be; I know I swallowed half of them as I ran through them with my mouth wide opened to yell at Joes. Dang gnats.

Pantin' from the run and sweat drippin' from my forehead, I grabbed my battered tin cup of sweet tea that Joes handed me and washed the gnats that got caught in my teeth all down with the first gulp. The tea was too good to just spit it out with the gnats. And 'sides, I rarely ever got tea at home.

Joes, he just laughed at me and tells me, "Little Anna, if yous would slow yous self down, yous would see the swarm of gnats and yous could go around them. Lowdy child, yous sweaty. Let's sit here for a few minutes while yous cool down and drinks your tea."

I laughed as Joes patted the top of my head. I done see him wipe his hand on his overalls after he touched my sweaty head. Joes, he always had the same shirt on. His shirt was gray and so thin I could see plum through it to his undershirt. One side of his overall snaps must have been broken, cause it was always hangin' unsnapped. His overalls had patches all over them. I wondered if they were as old as Joes? I didn't mind if Joes wore the same thing every day. His shoes were black boots that tied around his ankles; they were so worn they had white spots on them. I know what it's like to be made fun of for not havin' more than a couple of things to wear. 'Sides that's not what made me and Joes friends.

We sat on the porch silently for a while as we listened to the cicadas sing. A slight breeze finally began to blow and it brought with it the scent of pine from the trees that surrounded Joes place. There was a comfort in the silence between me and Joes. It was safe. Off in the distance I heard Joes rooster, Strut, crowin'. Joes, he started to hum. It started in his belly and then it reached his throat. I always waited for him to sing, but it always came out as a hum. He rocked in his rocker and the hum was in beat with the sound of the rocker. The cicadas decided to join in and I lay my head back against the post with my leg drawn up to my chest, wishin' this moment would last forever. There was somethin' sad about his hummin'. But I liked it anyways. It was like a big hug from Joes. Today, the cicadas seem to understand Joes' hummin'. 'Cause normally when I lay on my pallet at night, listenin' to them with the window opened, they are different. 'Cause when I close my eyes, I could see they sounds. They sounded like a million tiny rain drops filled with burst of sunrays that exploded when the raindrop found somethin' to land on.

Once I told my Momma I could see the sounds of what the cicadas sounded like and she said to me, "Anna Marie, if you would come out of that head of yours you might not get into so much trouble. You are so peculiar child; odd. I wonder how you ever came out of me."

But today, the cicadas sounded different. They sounded like they sunshine been taken away and they filled themselves up with the sound of Joes. Slow. Sad. Old. Lonely. Like they dunna got inside Joes' soul. Like they understood what he is hummin'. Wish I knew what he was sayin' inside the hum. He smiled at me. Wonder if that the only time he smiled; when he saw me. I reckon Joes, he needed love like me. That's why we was friends, 'cause we could sit in silence or with Joes hummin' and we knew the other one be there without sayin' a word.

I looked up at Joes. His head was laid back against his rocker and his eyes looked far in the distance. Joes, his mind wandered far away like my mind did. He looked sad. His black skin never seemed to sweat. Joes, he always smelled like lye soap; tellin' me how important it was for a person to be clean. I didn't mind a little dirt though. His head had almost no hair and what was there was white, like the tops of a cotton bush before it burst out completely with the cotton. But mostly, Joes, he wore his wide straw hat. It had a small hole in the back where he says a hummin' bird got stuck when it got too curious about him. When Joes smiled his teeth were so white. I never understood how someone's teeth and eyes looked so white like Joes. Joes, he shaved his face clean. He said his face should look like his head. I don't know what that means but sometimes I saw white on Joe's face, so I guess he be tellin' the truth. Joes, he never lied. Once I told Joes a lie about a grade I got at school. Joes, he got so upset with me and tells me, "Little Anna, don't yous be lyin'. Yous always tells the truth even if yous get in trouble. A person's word gotta mean somethin'." I don't know nothin' about a person's word, but I never told Joes a lie after that. I didn't like addin' sad to Joes eyes.

In the distant background I heard Bell and Star makin' noises for their food. Before I could say anythin', Joes, he stood up slowly and reached for the two buckets hangin' from a single nail on either side of the post where I was sittin' on the step. I was leanin' against one of the posts and I knew it was time to go feed the donkeys. I walked alongside Joes, tryin' to keep up with his big steps. Joes, he was tall, taller than my dad. His hands were big; I bet Joes, he could crush a watermelon if he be wantin' to. But they were gentle. I knows because he had tended my bruises for as long as I can remember. My Dad's hands were small but meaner than a snake. They could carry a punch. I know because I have been on the receivin' end of them.

Joes, he cleared his throat and said, "Little Anna, did I ever tell yous the story about Bell and Star?"

"no joes, i just reckoned they has been here as long as you have," I said. Joes, he gives a slight nod and what seemed to be a chuckle before he told his story.

"I comes upon a white man early ones mornin' on my ways to the grocery store to buy some cornmeal. This man, he was a beatin' those two donkeys. Them donkeys was cryin' and stampin' thems feet around somethin' fierce tryins to get away from the man's blows. He had him a big stick whackin' at them donkeys. His blow hit Star right between her eyes. Blood, it begins to gush out of the cut. The man raised his arm to gives her another strike but I stepped in fronts of the man. And I tolds him to put the stick down or I's would have to give him what he was givin' to them donkeys. The man he start cussin' at me and tellin' me hows stupid them donkeys were. That if I's didn't like the way he was treatin' them donkeys I could just buy them from him. I's only has me $2.45 to buy some cornmeal. I comes back home with Bell and Star and no cornmeal. This man, Little Anna, he be drinkin' from the bottle. No good comes when a man drinks from the bottle. Do yous understands me? Never be with a man who drinks, Little Anna." I nodded tryin' to follow what Joes was tellin' me, cause heck, the only men I knew was my Dad and brothers, and I knew what the bottle does to dad. So I guessed Joes was tellin' me to not be with

Dad either, cause ain't no good come from him. But Joes know I couldn't go nowhere when Dad drinks from the bottle. I just kept noddin' as Joes talked.

We poured the donkey's food into the pails and they come runnin' to the rail fence, nudgin' for the pails. I petted them as they ate and Joes told me more of the story.

"I's been takin' care of Bell and Star for near 18 years. I gives them a safe place to live. I tend them bruises and cuts that man gave them. I brings them back to health. I talks to them and feed them, Little Anna, the same way Jesus takes care of me. He brought me backs to my health. He showed me how to love, to forgive, to see the goods in people. Mans can be evil 'cause they don't know Jesus, yous understand, Little Anna?" I nodded again, cause I am wonderin' when Joes was sick and I didn't know. I shrugged my shoulders and thought about how there's some things I don't understand when Joes talks about his Jesus, but I liked his stories anyway.

"I calls Star her name 'cause of the scar in between hers two eyes. What that man dids to her, he left that scar shaped like a star. And Bell, her name comes from the bell I used to have tie around her neck. She would likes to wander off from the farm, but I always knows where she was because of the bell. Now she stays close to home and I knows where she is at all the time. She come to trust me, and now she knows I won't beat her, Little Anna. One day you will trust again. I promise."

Joes, he gots quiet after his story so we continued with the chores in silence. We both liked to have our own thoughts. As we walked passed Joes' garden that he planted next to the barn, we stopped and picked a few veggies, before feedin' the chickens and pumpin' water from the well to water Bell and Star. I wondered about the story Joes told me that day. Wonderin' how this Jesus teaches Joes. If He teaches Joes he must be really old, 'cause Joes, he done look like the oldest person in the world.

"Anna Marie!" I heard Momma callin' again.

"Go on now, Little Anna. 'Member what I tell yous today. Don't forget. Ya hears me?"

"i hears ya joes." I whispered back. Joes, he reached down and patted the top of my head. "joes, how come i can't stay with yous?" I fought back the urge to wrap my arms around Joes' neck. Maybe I can be like Bell. Joes could put a bell around my neck and he would always know where I was at. "joes, i ain't no different than bell and star. i get beatin's like them. maybe you can buy me for $2.45."

Joes, he shake his head and pointed in the direction of the house. "I be heres tomorrow, Little Anna. I be heres tomorrow. Goes along now before yous get in trouble." I stood there waitin', hopin' Joes would change his mind and I heard Momma again.

"okay, thanks for the tea and the story, joes." I said.

I let out a long sigh as I picked up my big stick to drag along side me as I walked back to the house. I felt safe draggin' that stick in case I ran across myself a snake. The smell of the pine seemed to follow me as a soft breeze brought some relief from the hot Alabama sun beatin' down on the sandy road. The sand burned the bottom of my feet but I didn't mind. We never had shoes in the summer. Daddy said they a waste of good money; buyin' shoes for youngun's feet in the summertime. I always wondered what it would be like to have shoes in the summer. I saw girls in town with sandals, some with sparkles on them. It reminded me of the stars sparklin' bright on a clear night. Nights I would lay out in the yard, wonderin' what life must be like for those girls. I bet they don't get beatin's froms they Daddy.

two

       I looked back and saw Joes standin' there as he watched me head home. Joes once told me that my blonde hair was lookin' like the silk that a caterpillar weaves. And my blue eyes, they looked like the sky just before sunset; a mix of dark and light blue. He said, "Little Anna, yous eyes be lookin' sad, but I knows one day your eyes will be filled with joy. One day, Little Anna, yous will finds the happiness that Jesus has for you."

       I didn't know nothin' about joy or happiness, but if Joes said one days I would have it, well I reckon, one days I would. Joes, he traced with his finger the freckles on my nose and cheeks and said it looked like someone took a paintbrush and placed each one of thems in just the right spot. I didn't like my freckles, but Joes said they had character. Joes, he be tellin' me thats I have power with people and that one day I will be famous. "One day, Little Anna, yous wills grow into that power and I hopes I am around to sees it." I just laughed at Joes and knowed he liked tellin' him stories and that was just part of his story tellin'. Joes, he always knew how to make me feel special and I wondered sometimes if he could be right. I wills remember to think on that when I needs somethin' to think on. He didn't seem to mind if my dress was a size too big or if it was dirty. He told me I dunna have a special place in his heart even though he knew it ain't right for a black man to be talkin' to a little white girl. I didn't understand why someones gotta know about who somebody's friend is or not. Joes seemed to understand how hard it was for me to go home and he stood there watchin' me until I turned the curve by the dark pink crepe myrtle. As the wind blew the branches they seemed to wave goodbye and it added to my sadness at leaving Joes' house.

I took my time walkin' back to the house. No needs to run. No one gonna be waitin' to smile at me or hand me a cold cup of tea. I thinks about Joes' story. The one 'bout Bell and Star and I think how lucky they were to have Joes; lucky like me. I saw the house from the distance and slowed down my walk even more. The back of the house looked like white squares stacked on top of each other with three steps that led up to a small screened porch. Two large pecan trees shaded the grassless back yard and brought some relief from the summer heat. Still, summer was my favorite time, 'cause I could spend every day, all day with Joes.

As I walked up the back stairs, I opened the screen door into the kitchen. I caught the smell of boil peanuts and I could hear Momma yellin', "Where have you been all day? You just wait until your Daddy gets home, he's gonna give you a beatin' for not doin' your chores today, missy, and that will not be my fault. I told you to do them, but you carry yourself off to only the good Lord knows where." Wishin' the sound of the radio would drown out her voice so I wouldn't have to listen to it, but Momma managed to be louder than Patsy singin' "Crazy". I looked at my Momma as she was yellin' at me; she was real pretty. I had heard manys of people say that about her. I stared at her from the corner of my eyes, waitin' to see if she was goin' to smile at me the way Joes does. She doesn't. I looked at her mouth, Momma she always wore red lipstick on her lips. The cigarette she was holdin' had her lipstick marks on it and when she drank her tea, hers glass always had her red lipstick left behind. As blue as my eyes are, my Momma's eyes were green. Theys a bright green like the leaves I found on the peonies. Hers hair was black, like Joes skin. She was tall, a little taller than my dad, and skinny. Hers hair was curly from the curlers she puts in her hair at night and it touched the top of her shoulders. Momma usually wore pants that zipped up at the sides, with flat shoes, so she didn't tower too much over my dad. He didn't like that. Momma, she kept talkin', but I tuned her out and I started thinkin's about tomorrow, and I couldn't wait for the sun to go down, so it will come up and I could leave the house again. I dropped my shoulders and hung my head to prepare for another long night of yellin', cussin', and beatin's and the "thing" that always seemed to happen. Momma, she snapped her fingers at me and I looked up at her as she was tellin' me to set the table for dinner. Momma's hands were nice; they looked soft and her fingernails were always painted red like her lips. I took out the plates from the cabinets and she called for Frannie to come help. Frannie is my sister. She was only 13 months older than me. Momma, she liked to dress us like twins, but we looks nothin' alike. Frannie, she had green eyes they were big and round like my Momma's and her hair was brown like mud you find in a puddle after a hard rain. Frannie was shy and quiet. She lets me do most of the talkin' when we gets around a bunch of people. Frannie walked in the room and gave me a smile. I smiled back at her. As I counted out the plates, I wondered why theys don't match like my Grammy's does. We got the table set and dinner on the table. Momma called for the other kids to come eat as Daddy walked in the door. I never really liked dinner time. We kids weren't allowed to talk. Daddy always said kids are to be seen, and not heard. Momma and Daddy, theys talk about their days and usually about other people's problems. I only like dinner 'cause my belly always seemed to be needin' food.

Daddy came home smellin' like fertilizer from workin' at the seed company. I hated that smell. It was a cross between animal manure and grass. Wished he would have had the decency to bathe and change before sittin' down at the supper table. Joes always says a person should be clean when theys eat. As we sat down to supper momma started chatterin' about how unruly the kids were today, and how I did not do my chores, as she looked at me with that "look". Sometimes I swear Momma hated me. There were eight of us kids. Why did she always pick on me? I was the one always gettin' the blame and the beatin's. I guess I was put here in the middle of all these youngun's cause somebody had to take the brunt of Daddy's anger. And it seemed Momma was content for it to be me. The radio was blarin' in the back-ground with Tammy Wynette, "I don't Wanna Play House" and Daddy was just eatin' his dinner, chewin' slowly as he looked down the table at me. Daddy was not a big man, just a little shorter thans my Momma. He had red hair and hints of blonde, and eyes so blue, like a clear sunny sky, they would be pretty if he were not so mean. He got his eye color from his Momma, my Grammy. I sometimes wondered why our eye color was so different, even though theys both be blue. I will remember to think on this when I be needin' somethin' to thinks on. His

~ 9 ~

hands had the same wrinkled look to them that my Grammy's had, even though he is not olds like Grammy. His eyes never seemed to look away from me. I pretended not to notice as I picked up my biscuit and took a bite. The biscuit was dry as I struggled to swallow it, knowin' what was comin'. The other kids were quiet as they too could feel it comin', and I can tell they were thankful daddy was not givin' them the look. I was in the middle of us kids. I had two older sisters, Nell and Frannie, two older brothers, Jack and Mike and three younger sisters, Diane, Molly and Shelly. It was nights like this that I wished I had never been born. I fought back a tear, but wasn't nobody gonna see me cry. I wouldn't cry.

I ain't quite figured out, I guess in my short eight years, why folks have kids if they don't even like them. I saw kids at school and they mommas be huggin' them and smilin' at them. Must be somethin' wrong with me I was thinkin'. Heck, I didn't even know what birthdays was until I walked into the classroom one mornin', saw my name on the blackboard and thought I was in trouble. Then, the teacher, she stood up and told the class it was my birthday and they sang, "Happy Birthday" to me. She said I could share with the class tomorrow what I gots for presents and what kind of cake my Momma and Daddy got me. The next day I told them I got a new doll and my Momma made a strawberry cake. I lied. Why teachers gotta be so nosey anyhows? I know Joes, he would be sad if he knew I dunna lied again. I ran home the day they sang happy birthday and announced to my Momma it was my birthday, and she said, "Anna Marie, you are not special and the day you were born I wanted to kill myself. The last thing I needed was another youngun' hangin' on me."

I jumped, startled as daddy said my name. I looked up and said, "Sir!"

"You heard me girl. I said get down on your hands and knees and lick up the food you dropped on the floor. You gonna eat like a dog, you can clean up your mess like a dog."

I was shakin' as I climbed out of my chair and got down on my hands and knees and began lickin' up the crumbs I dropped on the floor. Tears began to flow. The taste of dirt and crumbs mixed with the tears. I thought I would vomit, but knew if I did he would make me lick that up as well. But under my chair was not the only place my Daddy wanted me to lick. I had to lick the entire kitchen floor. A few kicks to my rear end from daddy's work boot, caught me off guard the first time, my face hit the floor givin' me a right smart bloody nose. All the while him tellin' me I was a worthless piece of crap and I was really gonna get the belt after I finished lickin' the floor clean. And I did. Blood was runnin' down my legs by the time daddy finished my beatin'. He said the beatin' was for makin' Momma worry about me after runnin' off and not tellin' her where I was. I wondered if Momma really cared about me, but it only lasted for one second as I saw her watchin' Daddy start the beatin's with a smile on her face as she lit up her cigarette.

Daddy sent me out to the garden field, after I finished the dishes, to pull weeds. Pullin' the weeds was for not doin' my chores. As I walked to the field in the dark, I was thankful for the full moon, cause Daddy said if I pulled up the vegetable plants I would get another beatin'. I looked up at the moon that illuminated the long rows of plants and I shuddered at the quiet night. A night owl began to hoot to let me know I wasn't alone. A person could thinks about a lot of things when they are left alone in the dark night. My mind began to wander as it usually did. I couldn't let my mind start makin' up scary stories about wild dogs surroundin' me and wantin' to eat me. "stop, anna marie!" I tells myself. "you have a long night ahead of yous and makin' up stories and gettin' sidetracked from your chore will not help yous."

Maybe I was crazy like Momma said. Maybe that is why my Daddy would get so mad at me and Momma didn't like me. I wish I could change whos I was, maybe then theys would love me. My mind was swirlin' with lots of things to think about, but I settled my mind on thinkin' about a new family as usual. I had this family in my minds, where the dad would picks me up and swings me in the air cause he was happy to see me at the end of his work day. A mom who combed my hair after my bath and a beds that was comfy, soft and warm.

I pulled weeds, daydreamin' and lookin' up at the moon and wonderin' about Joes' Jesus. Joes, he always had a story to tell. He always be tellin' me how God made the world. One time he said, "Little Anna, when yous look up at the stars, that is how much God be lovin' yous." I ain't be knowin' anythin' about that, but I did wonder sometimes why I couldn't feel His love. Joes, he made it sounds like God is with yous all the times. Wonder wheres He was tonight when I was gettin' my beatin'? I sure didn't feels no loves tonight, not evens from Joes' Jesus. I reckon, I don't really knows what love feels like unless my and Joes friendship is love.

I looked at the last row of butter beans and saw the crest of the sun peekin' over the treetops and knows a new day was about to begin. I couldn't wait to gets to Joes. I knows he would have some breakfast for me. I heard the sound of the screen door slammin' and I knew Daddy would be leavin' for his job. I waited to hear the work truck start and I could see the tail lights as Daddy turned onto the road. As I let out a long sigh, it felt like I had held my breath all night. The dust trail from his truck reached the edge of the pea row where I had just finished pulling the last of the weeds. I looked down at my hands and saw they were covered with dirt and green stain from the weeds. As I looked at them, my eyes filled with tears as the hole in my heart got bigger. I wondered as I always did, what was wrong with me?

three

I be thankful he did not inspect my work. I knew Momma wouldn't come check on me when she got up for the day so I ran as fast as I could back to sees Joes, with my stick in hand. This time, no gnats. Must be too early for thems to be up and swarmin' in one place. It was like Joes was waitin' for me. I ain't ever know how he seemed to know but there him was, he always had a nice smile. But his smile goes as quick as lightnin'; he frowns as I come nearer, "Lawdy, child, what done happens to ya?"

"it ain't nothin' joes." I forced a smile as I waved my dirty hand in the air. The truths be, I wanted to just sit on his steps and drink his sweet tea and hear his stories. I felt safe on his steps. I never was allowed to go inside his house, but this mornin' he said I had to; he needed to tend my bruises. He said they the worst he ever seen on me.

"Child, yous have on the same clothes as yesterday and yous dirty. Did yous not bathe last night?" I shared what happen. Joes, he tried to hide his tears but I seen them. He was extra careful not to rub the ointment too hard into the open wounds on my legs.

"oh heck joes, ain't no need to cry. one day I am gonna run away. one day I am gonna find a family that love me." I try to sound all brave and grown up so Joes wouldn't be so sad. But deep down inside my belly, I wondered if somethin' was wrong with me. Maybe I ain't that loveable. Maybe this was just what life was like. Long as I could remember, I was gettin' beatin's. Then Joes, he began to tell me another story about Jesus. He done told stories before about Jesus, but this was like He was magic or somethin'. "Just say in your mind what you need and he bring it to do." I think Joes done lost his mind. Old people they gets that way. Maybe Joes done got the old man disease. I ain't ever heard anybody talk about Jesus but Joes. He is ramblin' on and on, I tuned him out that day, I just needed to let my mind wander to the music. Listenin' to Joe's music in the background was different than what Momma listened to. Someone singin' a song about RESPECT. I could tell she was black by her voice and the music was different, rhythmic. She kept spellin' the word like that might help people know what she was singin' about.

I think Joes done know that I checked out cause he say in a stern voice, "Little Anna."

I say, "crap! joes, you done scare me!"

Joes, he gives me "that look" the one, where I know I had done and hurt him. His eyes got really sad; I don't like makin' Joes' eyes sad. He said to me in that stern voice that I had only heard a couple of times, "Little Anna, don't you be usin' cuss words like that. Yous a lady and ladies don't talk like that. Yous gonna be famous one day and yous have to learn to talk proper white lady talk. You can't talk like me or be usin' cuss words like yous Daddy use."

I said "okay joes, I won't use cuss words no more." It seemed so important to him for me to understand this. Ladies don't use cuss words. I wondered that day what it meant to be a lady. I made a promise to myself on that day, that I would find out what a lady was and why Joes wanted me to be one. But that would have to waits until later, my belly was hungry, and it began to talk to both Joes and me.

I was listenin' as Joes continued to talk about this Jesus. So halfway through one of his stories it dawns on me. I don't know where this Jesus lives. 'Cause I was thinkin' about goin' to see him. So I asked. The look on Joes face, I swear his black skin done turn almost white.

Joes looked at me all sad like and he said, "Little Anna, don't you know 'bout where Jesus lives? Ain't I told you that before?" I shake my head no. "He is our Savior. He lived right here on this earth, Him had to go to heaven fors awhile, but He gonna come backs one day and they won't be any more pain, or tears, or fightin'. Little Anna, I promise yous, His words are true and one day yous will have more than yous could ever dream, hope

~ 14 ~

or imagine. Yous have to talk to Him. He hears yous and He will give yous what yous ask for and He will protect yous, Little Anna, if yous ask Him into your heart." I just nodded, knowin' for sure poor Joes had gotten the old man disease.

There ain't nobody could ever protect me from Daddy's beatin's. Especially a man who didn't even live on this earth anymore. I let out a long sigh and wished this Jesus was real.

Joes, he finished puttin' the ointment on my belt marks and wiped the dried blood off my nose, mouth, and legs. He let out a long sigh and began to hum. He hummed when he didn't want to talk anymores. Joes, he sent me back to the front porch while he made me some bacon and eggs. I sat on the top step thinkin' about takin' a nap, but a bumble bee buzzed by my ear and landed on the rose bush next to the step I was sittin' on. It was having breakfast. I looked at that bumble bee and wished I could fly away, far, far away.

Lookin' out at Joes' yard, I saw that Strut was out of his pen, the early mornin' fog hadn't lifted yet, and the sun was peakin' through the moss that was hangin' from the trees. The smell of bacon began to ticklin' my nose remindin' my belly it was empty and my eyes were gettin' heavy. I needed to find a place to close my eyes. But before I could, Joes brought my plate of food. Joes knew how I liked my eggs: runny yolks spillin' over my grits, and as always they was cooked exactly like I liked. We sat there in silence. Strut crowin' and Bell and Star lettin' us know they were awake. Joe's farm was wakin' up and the daily chores were waitin' for Joes to take care of thems.

As we sat there I said, "joes, how comes my momma and daddy don't love me?" Joes, he reached to sat his empty plate beside him and let out a long sigh as he folded his hands over his belly.

He said, "Little Anna, yous momma and daddy they be lovin' you child. Theys just don't knows how to shows it sometimes. Yous Daddy, he disciplines you hard. Shouldn't no man beat a child that hards. And your momma, she, wells she just has a hard time showin' yous. Yous be rememberin' what I tells yous about my loves for ya. Yous remembers, child, hows specials you are. One days, Little Anna, yous will know."

I sat there and knows I gotta goes home, not because Momma would miss me, but because I need to find a place to close my eyes for a while. I don't think I have ever been so sleepy. My whole body felt sleepy.

Before Momma had a chance to start yellin' at me with all that frustration in her voice, I picked up my stick and headed back home. I thanked Joes for the ointment, the food, and the talk about Jesus. I figured I wouldn't let him know I knew he already was gettin' the old man disease; all that talk about Jesus givin' yous what yous wants and all. Maybe tomorrow I would spend the whole day with Joes.

As I was walkin' back home, that song that was playin' on Joes' radio was stuck in my head. "R-E-S-P-E-C-T". I guess she had a Daddy like mine. Women, they don't get respect. I may have only been 8, but even an 8 year old knew that was the way it was. Thinkin' about Joes, I let out a long sigh. Somethin' different about Joes story that day. He seemed like he really wanted me to understand somethin' but I was not sure what it would be.

four

Momma was on the telephone with someone talkin' about someone else. I heard her use a cuss word. Too bad Joes was not here, he could have given her "the look." I bet it would have made my Momma wished she hadn't cussed. Momma got off the phone and told me to wash the dishes from lunch. I climbed up on the stool to reach the sink and began to wash the dishes.

Momma came back in and said to me, "Anna Marie, I don't know why you bring the beatin's to yourself. If you would just listen and do your chores, you wouldn't upset your Daddy so." I just looked at her. Why was she even talkin' to me? As long as I could remember, all I ever wanted was for her to once tell Daddy not to beat me, and give me a hug and tell me everythin' was gonna be alright. I couldn't even remember Momma huggin' me. I wanted to remember, because I can't stand the thought of that being true; but I know it was. Momma snapped her finger at me and told me to listen, "You are always 100 miles away girl, I swear sometime I think you're short upstairs."

As she turned to walk away, she knocked off the glass pitcher; the Schlitz beer pitcher, Daddy's favorite. "Now look at what you have done, Anna Marie. Now you are gonna get it when your Daddy comes home."

I looked at her and began to protest, "but I didn't do it!"

"Don't you sass me young lady! I said you did it. If you hadn't distracted me I wouldn't have knocked it off. So you did it!"

About that time I heard Daddy pullin' into the driveway and his heavy boots on the porch. My heart started to race. I could hear Momma sayin' to him, "Anna Marie broke your Schlitz pitcher ...she was sassin' me back and distracted me, and caused me to knocked it off the counter. She is just a strange child." Daddy walked in, took his belt off and began to beat me in the same places as last night. I didn't think he would ever stop. I got dizzy and sick at my stomach. All I could think of was why Momma would tell him I did it; I guess she didn't want the beatin'. I kept hearin' the song, "Respect," I was thinkin' about Joes' story about Jesus; anythin' to make the pain go away. Finally he stopped and sent me to throw it away. When I came back, Daddy told me I had to take all the dishes and all the pots and pans out of the cabinets and wash them; my punishment for "breaking the pitcher" and no dinner, he added. And Momma made my favorite too; fried chicken with turnip greens and cornbread. She didn't make it because it was my favorite. I never told her. I was afraid she would stop makin' it if she knew it was my favorite.

By the time everyone was finished with their supper I had everythin' washed that was in the cabinets and drawers. My hands looked like a piece of meat left to dry and shriveled up, just like jerky. My legs were bleedin' from the beatin' and my stomach sounded like one of Joes donkeys. I was so hungry I could have eaten out of the garbage, which is what I did when I took the food scraps out to toss. Not much was left on the chicken bones, just enough to make me wish I had not missed dinner.

By the time I finished with the dishes, the other kids had their baths. I was the last one, so I got the tub of dirty water 'cause Daddy only allowed one tub of water to be run. This was the first house I remember livin' in that had runnin' water and a toilet inside. We used to relieve ourselves in an outhouse. We would bathe ourselves in pails of water. Even then I had to use someone else's bath water. You would think water was like gold or somethin' the way Daddy would go on and on, like he was afraid we might run out of water or somethin'. I always hated goin' last. I knew my brothers peed in the water; they was like that, mean like our Daddy. I hated sittin' in the tub of water, knowin' the boys had peed in it. Bad enough I got everyone else's dirt. I dreamed about the water falls Joes had told me about in his stories. I dreamed of washin' my body under them waterfalls; clean runnin' water that no one had peed in.

Momma came upstairs to tell me to get out and go to bed. So I put on the yellow dress that was a hand-me-down that I woulds be wearin' to school tomorrow and climbed into what I called bed. I shared a pallet with my sister, Frannie. She smiled as I layed next to her and I could tells she was sad for me. Frannie was always so nice and I think she was my Daddy's favorite. He was always tellin' her how pretty she was. Always takin' her for special rides in the car and tellin' her how smart she was. But the truth was I could spell better than she could. He never said nothin' about the papers I brought home with an A+ on them.

That night we laid there tryin' to fall asleep. It was so hot. No air was blowin'. The leaves on the trees were not movin'. The only thing comin' through the open windows was bugs. Sweat was seepin' through my clean dress and she said to me, "Annie?" I liked it when she called me that. No one else called me that but her. "Do you ever think about runnin' away? Daddy so mean to you." I held my breath, how did she know that I was goin' to run away?

"you aren't gonna tell on me are you?"

"No," she said. "If you do run away, take me with you." We made a pinky promise that night to run away together. I wondered why she would want to run away, cause Daddy is not mean to her. He was always so nice and smilin' at her all the time.

Deep into the night I could tell it was almost mornin' cause I could feel the dampness outside, like it gets just before the sun comes up. I felt someone lay down next to me. He put his hand on my mouth and told me I better not make a sound and that I better not tell anyone that he was in here. He began to do the "thing". I hated when he came into my room. I hated the "thing" he did. It made me sick. Once I tried to tell Momma and she slapped me in the face and called me a liar and a trouble maker. She said if I ever said anythin' to anyone she would turn Daddy loose on me. I guess that was why she smiles when Daddy beats me; she thought I deserved it for tellin'.

The next mornin' was the first day of school and I couldn't wait. There were so many kids, kids laughing and joking around. I overheard stories about vacations, birthday parties, sleepovers and shopping. They seemed so happy, like they lived in a fairy tale or somethin'. I loved seein' the girls, their hair was so shiny and they had pretty bows and socks that matched their dresses. I guess I didn't have friends 'cause my clothes were too big and they didn't match. Once I heard a girl say I smelled like pee as she and her friends walked away laughing. Darn bath water. I had to figure out a way not to be the last one to bathe when we had school.

I had a good first day in the 3rd grade. I was sittin' next to a pretty girl named Betsy. She lived in a big fancy house and her Momma brought her to school. She did not have to ride the bus. You could tell her Momma loved her good and she was always clean lookin'. I wondered how she did that. She smiled all the time and all the kids wanted her to be their friend. I thought about her as I rode the school bus home. I am sure she did not have a list of chores to do when she got home and she was not afraid her Daddy's gonna beat her either.

She got RESPECT. I smiled. One day I will have respect too.

five

No one was home so I ran to the back of the property to tell Joes about my day. He always wanted to know. He asked all kinds of questions like he was interested in me and how I felt about this and that. Joe was sittin' on his front porch. I wondered why Joes wasn't standin' waitin' for me with a glass of cold tea. I guessed he must be tired today. I ran a little faster excited to see him, but only he wasn't lookin' at me. His head was down, like he was asleep. I slowed my run down to a walk, wonderin' why Joes was so still. My heart was beatin' fast, but I didn't thinks it's from the runnin'. I could feel somethin' was wrong, really wrong. My mind wanted me to keep runnin'; but my legs felt so heavy, like I couldn't put one in fronts of the other. I called his name, but he didn't move. I walked up the stairs all the whiles callin' his name.

"joes, joes!" I reached my tremblin' hand to touch Joes. I put my hand on his shoulder and shook it a little but he did not move. He was holdin' the black book he reads out of about Jesus. I saw a note that had my name on it. I guessed I never wondered if Joes could write; I just supposed he couldn't. I kept sayin' "joes" but he did not wake up. I think the old man disease got him. I looked at him for the longest time, tears streamin' down my face. He was so black. His hands were huge, rough, like they seen a lot of hard work in his time; yet they were gentle enough to take care of my bruises. His face had white on it, like his head. I guessed Joes forgot to shave. I reached up and touched his cheek as tears began to fall. I rubbed his hand and told him I loved him. I never told him that before. I had never used those words to another human and I don't thinks I had ever loved anyone. My heart felt like it was gonna break. I used the back of my hand to wipe away the tears and snot as I picked up the note with my name on it and sat down on the front porch steps.

I read:

Little Anna, I know it wrongs for a black man to love a little white girl, but yous likes my daughter. I ain't no longer here to put ointment on your bruises yours Daddy give you. I goes ahead and be with Jesus. I want to see yous one day in Heaven. That is where Jesus lives, Little Anna, so yous talk to Jesus and ask Him into your heart. I know yous not be understandin' what I am talkin' about but yous keep this letter and yous take my black book and yous be readin' in it. Go to church, yous hear me now? Remember what I tell yous. Yous are a lady, so don't ever let anyone tell yous different and yous talk like a lady too, no cussin'. Bye now.

This had to be the saddest day of my life. My whole body shook while I cried and Joes wasn't here to hum, or to tell me a story or tell me it would be okay.

Since Joes didn't shave that day, I wondered if he fed the donkeys. I took the pails that were hangin' on the nails and headed out to the shed to fill them with the donkey food. I walked slowly over to where Star and Bell were and as they nudged their heads into the pails to eat, I told them that Joes was gone. He be with that Jesus he always be talkin' about. They seemed to knows that somethin' wasn't right. It was like Joes whole farm was sad. I stood there and looked around and knew my life would never be the same. I couldn't tell no ones about Joes. I stood in the middle of Joes' farm and felt my knees give way. Everywhere I looked, I saw Joes' love, in the way he took care of Star and Bell, and his veggie garden. I slowly made my way back to the porch one more time. I looked at Joes; my belly felt so empty like it does when I don't got no food in it.

"joes?" I whispered as my eyes filled with tears again and fell onto my dress. I reached up and wrapped my arms around Joes' neck and hugged him; I kept whisperin' his name as tears fell on top of his head, hopin' he would open his eyes. He didn't.

I picked up my big stick and began draggin' it beside me, darin' for a snake to crawl out in front of me. If Daddy spanked me that night I might have to hit him back. RESPECT. I kept hearin' that song in my head. I kept hearin' Joes humming the black folk songs. Somethin' soothin' about his music. I missed him already. I hid his note and book. I would be back to get it later. The walk home seemed longer than usual. I saw my favorite bird, the blue bird, but it couldn't even bring a smile to my face. My whole body was sad, it hurt, almost like I had gotten' a beatin'.

At home the kids were talkin' all at once like their day was more important than the other one. I sat down on the floor and began my homework. I couldn't tell anyones about Joes. I didn't want another beatin' for being back there. Grandpa went back to the end of the property once a week to check on him; he would find him. Poor Joes. I realized Joes would be alone, just sittin' there and I be wonderin' if I should have told Momma and Daddy...if another beatin' would be worth it and I knew Joes, he wouldn't want me to get in trouble so I kept quiet.

At dinner Momma kept lookin' at me, like she knew somethin' was wrong but she didn't ask. I wouldn't tell her anyway. I guessed she thought the "thing" was happenin' again. She would be right, but that wasn't what was makin' my heart hurt.

Somehow I got last bath again that night, darn peed water. Darn brothers, meaner than a snake. Both of them liked to go around beatin' on us. I guessed cause they seen Daddy doin' it.
Momma never said anythin', just let it happen.

I couldn't wait to run away to find a place to close my eyes.

six

Some of the kids brought their lunch from home. I always wondered how they got so much love from their parents. At lunch the next day, I saw the girl that sat next to me in homeroom had some orange things; I later learned they were cheese puffs. After lunch, we all got settled in and the teacher began the lesson. We were workin' on cursive writin'. I liked to learn it. It made me feel special to write cursive. Daddy didn't know how to. I guess in a way it made me feel more special than him. We all got up to wash our hands for a snack and Betsy left her desk top open; I just could not help myself. I took those cheese puffs and darn near ate them before she came back. She looked at me and her half empty bag and began to cry and told Mrs. Black I stole her cheese puffs. I had to go to the principal's office and I gots a paddlin' and a note pinned to my dress for Momma and Daddy. I had to bring it back with a note from them that the problem was taken care of. I dreaded the school bus ride home. Now, I felt bad for stealin', but I have to admit I have never tasted anythin' like that; they just kinda melted in your mouth and left this cheesy build up on your teeth. I could still taste them. We never got store bought anythin'. Momma made everythin' we ate from scratch and it came off our farm. Daddy wouldn't eat in restaurants. He didn't like milk and butter and he thought everyone was out to get him. This was always a fight in our house, cause Momma she liked milk and butter, she was raised eatin' and drinkin' dairy. But Daddy won, as usual, so no milk or butter in our house. I think the real reason he didn't want to eat in a restaurant was because he didn't have proper learnin'.

The bus driver let us off at the end of the road and we would walk the rest of the way home. I always left my big stick lyin' under the pecan tree; I swear that tree was the biggest tree I had ever seen, must've been here since them dinosaurs. I always had my big stick. The other kids made fun of me until one day walkin' home a big rattler was stretched over half the width of that sandy road. I took my stick and whacked it several times until it quit movin'. They never made fun of my big stick again.

At home, Momma was packin' like crazy. Boxes everywhere. She began yellin' at us the minute we walked in the door.

"Pack your stuff! What you don't have packed before your Dad gets here, stays." It was easy for me; I only had 4 dresses, one pair of new shoes for school, two outfits to change into after school, and three pairs of panties. Done.

The other kids were tryin' to figure out why we were leavin' in the middle of the school year and where we were goin'. I didn't care since I didn't have to give Momma and Daddy my note from the principal. It was one secret that was mine to keep and one beatin' I avoided. I didn't really care where we were movin'. I tossed the note into the trash.

While everyone else was busy packin', I ran to the back of the property to get the note and book Joes left me. I hadn't been back there since I found him dead. I stopped short of the front porch half expectin' him to be standin' there with a cup of cold tea, waitin' for me with a big smile. No one ever mentioned Joes dyin'; I hoped Grandpa gave him a proper burial. I walked to the pen to see if Star and Bell needed feedin', but theys gone. Joes' chickens were gone. I walked up to the porch and saw the pails hangin' where Joes had always put'em. Joes' chair was there, waitin', it seemed, for Joes. I sat on the stairs and stared at Joes' chair. I sighed and closed my eyes. If Joes was still here, he would be tellin' me not to be afraid of change. "Change was goods, Little Anna." He would be tellin' me to remember: talks like a lady, be nice, be polite, says thank yous, don'ts be lyin', and always tells the truth. I's be here when yous get backs. But you won't be Joes, yous dunna gone. I am gonna miss yous Joes. I wanted to stay. Joes was the only things I could count on. Now what, I wondered? I shivered, like a cold wind had touched my skin.

I found where I had hidden the book and note and raced back home. I put the note inside the book and buried it in the bottom of my brown paper bag that had my clothes in it. Daddy was loadin' the car with our personal belongin's and we were headed to Illinois, just like that.

We left all our furniture and pots and pans and dishes. I ain't ever seen anythin' like it. But this would be one of many moves like this for us; back and forth, from Illinois to Alabama and back again.

Eight of us kids sandwiched into the back seat, Momma and Daddy in the front seat. They always be lightin' up a cigarette. Don't they knows I couldn't breathe when they smoked? I hated cigarettes. The radio was on, playin' country music, it always sounded so sad and someone was always cheatin' on someone. I missed Joe's black music and would play it in my head, drownin' out the sound of Connie Smith singin' "Once a Day". Why do country singers always sing about someone lovin' them, breakin' their hearts and beggin' them to come back so they can do it all again? Maybe they would be better off singin' the black lady song "RESPECT".

I had to relieve myself but Daddy wouldn't stop until we needed gas. He said, "You mention it again, missy, and I will give you the belt." I hated my life. Why grownups always makin' decisions for you? Like they knew how long you could hold your pee. My belly was hungry and rumblin' like a train comin' down the tracks at midnight. It was hot and we were all sweatin'. The kids were ill-temper and started complainin'; we had been in the car near 3 hours. Finally we stopped. Daddy got gas, and bought himself a soda water. My mouth watered. I wanted a taste so badly. But Momma had packed water jugs for us kids along with vienna sausages and crackers for our supper. I finally got to relieve myself. Daddy said we were drivin' all night. We piled back into the car and I tuned everyone out. "There Goes my Everything" by Jack Greene blarin' on the radio. Stupid country music. The kids were fussin' back and forth and Momma actin' like she was so happy we just up and left everythin'. I guessed cause we were goin' to be around her people. I fell asleep, needin' to relieve myself and thinkin' of Joes. I missed him and wondered what it would be like to lives in another state. About as awful, I guess, as livin' in Alabama.

I woke up to the radio still blarin' and cigarette smoke fillin' the car. I told Daddy I needed to relieve myself and he said I missed the last stop and had to wait until the next stop.

"how long?" I ask.

"Stop that fussin', missy! We will stop when I say we stop!" Here we go again, a grown-up tellin' you how long you could hold your pee. Seemed like all I could think about was peein'.

The other kids began wakin' up and we finally pulled over to the side of the road and relieved ourselves. I noticed the trees were different here. I guessed we were in Illinois. There were no pine trees and it felt cooler. I shivered, wonderin' what our new life would be like and what Momma's people were like. I guessed I met them, but was too young to remember. Momma took food out of the bags for our breakfast and it was the same as we had for supper: vienna sausages and crackers. I guess I should be thankful, but I about had my fill of vienna sausages and crackers. My belly wanted grits and eggs. I wondered if they had grits in Illinois. I wondered if my life would be different there, as I allowed myself to be filled with hope.

We drove only for a short while before we pulled into a drive-way that led to a small white house with black trim. My belly hurt; in part not knowin' what these people were like, that and the lack of food.

Momma's Momma came runnin' out the house like she was a crazy woman. A robust woman, with black hair like my Momma's, arms a flingin' into the air like she swattin' away mosquitoes. She seemed real happy to see momma. My momma cried and laughed at the same time. I thought everyone done lost they minds. I just stood in the background watchin' all of this unfold and somehow sensin' in my gut...this ain't gonna be good. Sometimes I could sense things before theys happen. Joes, he told me that's the Holy Spirit. I don't know nothin' about that, but my hope began to fade as the hair on the back of my neck was standin' straight up and I was pretty sure it had nothin' to do with the cool breeze.

seven

"Annnnnnnna!" I heard one of my brothers callin' for me. I wish he would leave me alone. We had only been here four months. My birthday had already passed and no one said a word to me about it, but I was keepin' note of it. I had me a calendar and I marked the date of my birthday in red. I put a line through the other days. On the day of my birthday, I dreamed all day about what kinds of cake my new family would have for me. I would wear a new birthday dress and have a present to open.

"Annnnnnnnnnnnnna!" My brother called my name again. I was determined to stay hidden.

I didn't think I had ever been so cold in my life. We didn't have coats. Daddy said we could not afford them. He blamed Momma and said it's all her fault that we up and moved. He couldn't seem to find a job, but I was thankful he left early and didn't come back until late. I was not sure what he did, but one night durin' one of many fights, I heard Momma call him a cheater, yellin' at the top of her lungs about her brother's wife. Daddy yelled back that my momma was a cheater too; I heard my Daddy say he didn't even know how many of us kids was his; bastards, that's what he called us. I wondered if I was my Daddy's. Maybe that's why he looked at me sometimes with that look, like he hated me. I covered my ears hopin' to drown them out. Theys just some things a kid doesn't want to hear. I wished I was back at the farm; I missed Joes, his smilin' face, his gentle hands, even his words about Jesus echoed in my head. I wondered if I should get out his book again and try readin' it. I couldn't understand a word on the pages.

I reached for it, holdin' it, knowin' Joes touched it, that brought me comfort. One of Joe's favorite stories was about when he first saw me. I guess I was all but 4. I was sittin' in the middle of the watermelon patch at the back of the farm tryin' to crack open the biggest watermelon in the field. I was so hungry. It was hot and the next thing I know, this big black man is reachin' down with a knife in his hand. I hollered, he hollered, and said to me, "Now Little Anna, I ain't gonna hurt you. I gonna help you cut yous watermelon."

"Annnnnnnaa!" My brother hit me so hard my head fell back against the wall. "I been callin' and callin' you, you stupid girl. I said it is time for you to go out and feed the chickens."

"That is your chore, not mine, besides, it is freezin' outside." My brother dragged me out of my hidin' place. Joe's book fell to the floor and I was thankful he didn't notice it. I couldn't believe he found me; dang it, no one had for the last four months. Now I had to up and find a new place to hide. I yelled for him to let me go, but he dragged me down the stairs. Thump, thump, thump my body went as it hit every wooden step. I knew I would have bruises from the thumps. Seem my body always had bruises on it, either from my brothers or my Daddy. I finally hit the last step and as I tried to catch my breath, my brother grabbed my hair draggin' me to the back door.

I gave up and finally said, "ok, ok, i will feed the dang chickens." I wanted to cuss so badly, but remembered my promise to Joes, so I didn't.

I stumbled to put on summer shoes that I got for school in Alabama. They were hardly fit for this weather, but daddy's rule of one pair of shoes for the year, still held true here. I stepped out into the cold bitter wind and it went right through my summer dress, wishin' I had put my shorts on underneath it for added warmth. The snow swirled around in the air not really findin' a place to fall. It just seemed to be floatin' and floatin' until the wind picked it up and carried it high up in the sky and took it someplace else. I wished the wind would carry me away. I did not realize my brother had been watchin' me, until his fist landed upside my head.

"Girl, it is just like Momma said, you are short upstairs. Your mind is always somewhere else. Now, get the corn for the chickens and quit day dreamin'." Why men think they gotta control when you take a step or get corn for the chickens or relieve yourself was beyond me. I watched my brother as he left to go back to the house and I wondered if they be a good hidin' place out here somewhere. I'd rather be with the chickens than inside that house anyway. I couldn't wait to run away. I thought about that all the time; anyplace had to be better than this. I found myself thinkin' about Jesus. If He everythin' Joes said He was, I wondered why Jesus would put me with a family that didn't even like me. The only family that even seemed like they liked me was my Daddy's Momma. My mind drifted again.

I was not sure what a Grammy and Grandpa was supposed to be like. Momma, she didn't like my Daddy's Momma, so I didn't get to see her very often when we lived in Alabama. But when I did, she always smiled at me like she was sorry for somethin'. I had blue eyes like my Grammy's, but she had red hair and I had blonde. Her skin was so white like it never seen the sun and her hands was full of wrinkles. I wondered often when I would see her hands if you could unfold them wrinkles but I never been close enough to touch them. She would wear big hats on her head and gloves on her hands when she tended her flower gardens. She was known for her gardens. My favorite flowers was the hydrangeas and the peonies. I would sneak to her place sometimes on my way to Joes and watch her small body all bent over her flowers, tenderly touchin' and prunin' each one and wonderin' what it would be like to get a hug from her. I remembered her givin' me a peach after one of my Daddy's beatin's. He beat me in front of all my aunts and uncles and cousins. We were at my Grammy's havin' a family supper and I had spilled grape kool-aide on the floor (which I was disappointed because that was a big treat to have kool-aid, and I didn't even get to take a sip), and for that I was humiliated in front of my entire family. But she came out to the front porch where I was ordered to sit without lunch until it was time for us to leave.

She softly whispered to me, "Hang in there, Anna Marie, hang in there." And then before I knew it, she handed me a peach and then left to go back to the kitchen. I wanted to run after her, but fear of my Daddy kept me from it. I guess that was the closest I come to a hug. I ate that peach in record time, fearful it would be taken away.

Now, my Momma's Momma, well she was not like my Daddy's Momma at all. She was tall, with black hair and green eyes. My Momma looked like her except my Momma's slim, and she, well she fat.

And that is really all I have to say about her.

eight

I was walkin' back to the house and my brother raced up behind me and started to drag me back toward the chicken house.

"what are you doin'?" I yelled. Before I knew it, he had me by the electric fence used to keep the cows in place and made me grab it, while he peed on it. I thought I was goin' to die. All I could hear was him laughin'. The next thing I knew, I was wakin' up on the ground with him standin' over me, peein' right on my legs. My hands were burnin', as big welts began to show themselves in all their fury.

"Yous better not tell anyone about this, weirdo!" He said as he was zippin' up his pants still laughin'. I wished he would get it caught in the zipper, I found myself thinkin' as I watched him run back into the house. Where was Jesus I wondered? I didn't believe Joes' stories, because Jesus had not taken me away from this place. He had not given me a new Momma and Daddy who loved me. I thought He was supposed to give you what you ask for? I asked every night for Him to carry me away, like I saw the wind carry the snow, to the perfect place before the wind lets it fall. But I woke up every mornin' on the pallet next to my sister, Frannie. I guess He only like people like Joes, since Joes is with Him. Maybe He too busy listenin' to Joes? Because Joes, he can tell them stories. Jesus was lucky to have him. I wondered how Joes got there?

I walked back into the house freezin' and my hands burnin' like someone stuck a brandin' iron to them. I was tryin' to forget the pee that seemed to have turned into little ice cubes on my legs. I heard Momma comin' into the house.

I had tears on my face and she walked into the kitchen where I was and looked at me and said, "Not now Anna Marie. Whatever it is, suck it up. I have had a horrible day and your Daddy's right behind me, expectin' me to cook his supper. Anna Marie, take the potatoes out of the cellar and peel them for me like a good little girl."

I made my way down to the cellar. I hated it down there. There was dirt on the floor and several small rooms off to the side; there were shackles still attached to the walls. Story was, this house used to be a carriage house back in the day when people rode horses. They didn't have cars yet, and the rooms were where they would shackle the prisoners and slaves while the police would eat their meals upstairs. I thought about Joes and wondered if he were ever a slave, breaks my heart thinkin' about it. I hoped he wasn't. One day maybe I will ask my Grammy in Alabama to tell me about Joes, where he came from and why he didn't have kids. I had so many questions.

I made my way back upstairs with Momma's potatoes. Daddy had made it home and they were fightin' again about Mommas family comin' over after supper. I swear those people were over here all the time. Always big parties with lots of drinkin' and "things" happenin' that even a 9 year old knew was wrong. I was washin' the potatoes and the water burned my hands. Tears came to my eyes. I didn't want anyone to see me cryin' so I sucked it up like Momma said to and finished washin' and peelin' the potatoes. I put the potatoes in a pot of water and turned on the gas stove.

Momma, she looked like she was the one day dreamin'. She be looking extra special that night. Her hair was up on top of her head and her face looked different, like she might have had on more than just lipstick. Momma and I finished cookin' supper in silence, wishin' she woulds ask me what happened to my hands, but she didn't.

Supper time was awful that night. Momma and Daddy was goin' at it like they were tryin' to win a word contest. One would say somethin' and then the other just could not hold they tongue and had to spout out another word. Hateful words to one another; it made my tummy hurt. Didn't they know a kid can't enjoy their food when they parents fight like that?

Just as I was about to take another bite of my boiled potatoes, I heard daddy's chair hit the floor as he jumped up to take a swing at my Momma. I can't remember my Daddy ever hittin' her; only just yellin' and cussin' all the time, but never hittin' her. My Momma's chair hit the floor hard as she ducked before Daddy's hand could land on her. Daddy, he was cussin' all the while walkin' up the four stairs that lead into the livin' room. My momma, she grabbed a knife out of the drain board that was sittin' next to the sink, then she followed Daddy up them stairs. We kids just sat there for a moment, my bite of potatoes frozen in mid-air trying to understand what just happened, before we realized my Daddy was yellin', "Don't kill me woman!" We jumped up and ran into the room, I saw Momma standin' over him with the knife up in the air. We kids began to yell at her not to do it. We were cryin' and shoutin', runnin' around in circles. I guess 'cause we didn't know what else to do. My Momma she done have that look in her eyes you see when a dog get rabies. She dunna gone plum crazy. I closed my eyes, I didn't want to see her kill my Daddy. Even though I reckon I hated him, I didn't want to see him dead either. All I could think about was, I would have to clean up the mess. I guess that's how kids think. The phone ringin' made my eyes pop open as I saw Daddy grabbin' it to answer. He sounded all calm like as he started talkin' to my Momma's Momma, tellin' her that my Momma was holdin' a knife on him. He handed Momma the phone as he told us kids to shut up our cryin' and screamin'. I heard Momma talkin' and she began to smile as she put the knife down to her side and I heard her sayin', "Ok, we will see you after a while."

And that was that. Just like that, it was over.

My stomach hurt so much I thought I was going to vomit, and as for Momma, well she acted like nothin' ever happened as she got ready for her big party with her family. I thought about Momma as I headed back to the kitchen; somethin' not right with that woman. Maybe she done need a pill I heard one of the kids talk about at school. They Momma's take to keep from being crazy. I shuddered. I hope I didn't get the crazies. I went back to the kitchen and looked at that bite of boiled potatoes, wishin' I could have finished my supper. I was ordered to help clean up the dishes before everybody got here. Nobody seemed to notice I missed more meals than I ever got to eat. I guess just as well, my belly was all nervous inside anyway, and it seemed my heart was beatin' in the palms of my hands where the welts from the fence would not let me forget the events of the day.

As everyone arrived, I stepped out of the room headed to my new hidin' place, but Daddy saw me and told me, "Anna Marie, your Momma gonna need your help tonight. Just find yourself a corner to sit in until you are needed. Go on now, sit, and stay there until I tell you to go to bed." His boot landed on my backside as I walked away. I thought Daddy's boots landed on my backside more than they ever saw the dirt.

It seemed these adults didn't know how to do anythin' for they self.

I got orders like, "Girl, get me another bottle of beer. Girl, empty out those ashtrays. Take out the trash, girl, can't you see it is full?" I bit my lip so I would not sass back. I didn't even know these people and I certainly didn't like them. Joes, he told me I should try to like everybody, but I knew deep in my heart even Joes would not approve of what happen at these parties. The least these people could do was call me by my name; it isn't "girl". I longed for the porch steps at Joes'house. I didn't think anyplace could be as bad as Alabama, but I think being here for just a short while, I had found it.

As I tried not to choke on the cigarette smoke that soon filled the room, I took it all in. The record player was stacked with records as they dropped one by one, with the needle gettin' caught every once in awhile, repeatin' the same words over and over until one of the adults walked by and moved it. Grown-ups split into smaller groups with some goin' into other rooms and some put on their coats and went outside. They were laughin' and talkin' and didn't seem to mind they conversations weren't fit for a 9 year old to hear. I settled into my corner, pullin' my knees up to my chin and wrappin' my arms around my legs for an endless night of bein' ordered around and waitin'. Just waitin'...knowin' what was comin'. I let out a big sigh as I put my head down, drownin' out everythin' else around me as I let my mind return to the thought of when I met Joes for the first time in that watermelon patch.

When I think back and try to remember the first thoughts of my life, Joes is the first memory I have. I guess that is because he was the only person that was nice to me. You would think it would be my Momma or Daddy. I guess I remember them after I have memories of Joes, but those memories are not good ones. Joes, he knelt down to help me with that watermelon and he cut it wide open with one slice of his knife. I don't think I have ever eaten a watermelon any sweeter, and I remember my belly

~ 35 ~

needin' food. Guess that is why I made my way down to the back of the field. I was lookin' for food. I looked up at Joes and he smiled all big. I reckon I should have been scared, but there's somethin' about Joe's smile that let me know it was okay to be here with him. I pushed the other half of the watermelon over to Joes and said "eat". Joes, he just laughs, not a loud laugh, it was kinda like under his breath. I remember thinkin' it was a nice sound. He started to eat his half of the watermelon. He spit out his seeds. They seemed to land in the same place and as I dug into my half, the juice from the sweetness ran down my arms and dripped onto my legs. I got all sticky as I ate, tryin' to spit my seeds in the same place as Joes spit his; but they missed and with every try, I saw Joes smile. Before long, my belly was full.

Joes, he looked at me and said, "Little Anna, I been watchin' you since you moved here last year. I reckon you be about 3 then. You always walkin' back here by yourself. So I takes it upon myself to be your watcher." I looked at Joes and he knew I didn't understand all he was sayin'.

"My name is Joe," he said, "but it's best you don't say my name to anyone, just to me, you understand?"

I nodded and said, "hi, joes."

He smiled and said, "Now listen, Little Anna, you walks back here all the time by yourself. You need somethin' to protect yourself in case you run across a snake or somethin', so I want you to carry this here stick. Keep it with you every time you leave the house, you understand me?"

I nodded. I picked up the stick, and it was as big as me. I wondered how I was supposed to carry it? Joes, he just laughed when he saw me holdin' it; he showed me how to drag it behind me and up until we moved, I carried that stick every day.

"Girl!" I heard someone callin' me. I looked up wishin' I could stay lost in the memory of Joes and his kindness forever. I wanted to be in heaven with Joes. Wonder if I had to die to be in heaven? Wish Joes was here so I could ask him. I bet he still had a hold of Jesus' ears; maybe that is why I was still here. Joes won't quit talkin'.

"Get me another beer and don't be slow about it." I look toward the man who barked the order to fetch him a beer and realized it was my Momma's brother. I shot him a furrowin' of my eyebrows and lips pinched together, lettin' him know I wasn't happy about being told what to do.

I did as I was told, but instead of returnin' to my corner, I slipped outside to catch a clean gulp of air. The air was so cold I could see my breath, but I didn't mind. I had on the same dress as that mornin' but I remembered to add my shorts for extra warmth. I grabbed a pair of socks and put them on my hands so my fingers wouldn't start to tingle. Then wrappin' my arms around my body, I hoped I could stand the cold until everyone left. I walked around toward the back of the house and saw that the full moon was sittin' right over the pond givin' it the appearance of sparkles on top. The snow was softly fallin', and for the first time that night I found peace in my belly. Except for spendin' time with Joes, I guess I liked bein' alone where my mind could wander anywhere it wanted to. I could think about anythin' I wanted. No one could take that from me. I thought about Momma, and the crazy look she had in her eyes. I thought about Daddy's beatin's and my brothers' meanness. I thought about Momma's family and how different they were. I found me a place to sit out by the pond and watched the snow begin to fall a little heavier and wondered if it snows in heaven. Before we moved here I ain't never seen snow before, heard Momma talkin' about it, but never seen it. It's okay I guess, but it doesn't take the place of Joes front porch.

I jumped up, hearin' voices comin' at me; guess I must have fallen asleep. My clothes were wet, covered with snow and I realized how cold I was. I climbed up to the lowest branch on the tree and settled myself in the crook of the branch so they could not see me. I made out the two comin' toward me; it was my Momma and a friend of one of my uncle's. He had his arm around her waist, and she was leanin' her head into his shoulders. She looked up at him and they kissed. I just about fell out of the tree. Why, Anna Marie, I asked myself, do you always end up in the wrong place? This was one of the reasons I hated these parties. This place, Momma's people, the grown-ups always doin' things they shouldn't. They started touchin' each other. I closed my eyes. I didn't want to be there. I didn't want to see her do these things. I shouldn't be here I was thinkin', but didn't want Momma to know I was there.

About that time I sneezed and she dunna heard me.

"Who is that? Anna Marie, is that you, girl? What are you doin' out here? You are supposed to be in the house in your corner. Get down here, right now!"

~ 37 ~

She grabbed me at the back of my hair and pushed me so hard I fell on the ground. "Get your butt back to the house, and if you say a word to your Daddy, well, he will give you the belt for not being in your corner."

"okay, momma, i won't say a word." I picked myself up off the ground and ran back toward the house, sneezin' and coughin' all the way. I was wipin' tears off my cheeks before they have a chance to freeze. I wasn't cryin' cause I got hurt when I fell, I was cryin' cause I hated my life.

"joes?" I said out loud. "can you hear me joes? i need you joes. send me your jesus joes. i have nowhere to go." I cried. I guess I ain't never felt so alone and forgotten.

Instead of goin' back to the house like momma said, I went to the chicken house. I found myself some straw, made myself a bed and lay there. No one was goin' to notice anyhow. They were all good and drunk by now. I started thinkin' and thinkin' and my mind would not stop thinkin'. Why am I here? Why did Joes die? Why won't Jesus take me away? Why am I alive? As I cried myself to sleep, the last thing I remember thinkin' was how alone I felt. How empty it was without Joes. I woke up with the sun comin' in the chicken house and the rooster crowin' like its crower was stuck.

"shut up!" I yelled. "don't wake everyone up!" I jumped up and ran into the house hopin' I was the first one up. If I was the first one up and could get a head start on the cleanin', maybe Daddy wouldn't remember I didn't stay in my corner last night. The house still had cigarette smoke clingin' to the ceilin'. Ash trays runnin' over, beer bottles sittin' around everywhere, and a couple of people asleep on the floor. I tip-toed around pickin' up the beer bottles, cleanin' out the ashtrays, emptyin' out the trash cans, and washin' up the dirty dishes. I made coffee, started the bacon, and then I busied myself makin' biscuits. I guess the smell of the coffee dunna woke up Momma and Daddy. They came stumblin' into the kitchen. Momma reached for two cups and poured her and Daddy cups of coffee.

She looked at me, "Anna Marie, thanks for makin' the coffee."

I nodded at her afraid to speak, ours eyes locked on each other, and we had an understandin' that mornin'. My Momma and me. I wouldn't say anythin' about what I saw last night and she wouldn't tell Daddy I didn't stay in my corner. Odd, I suppose, but in some way, at that moment, she needed me.

After that party, the only fight I heard Momma and Daddy have was about a Christmas tree. Momma wanted one and Daddy didn't. We had never had a Christmas tree. On our way over to Momma's Momma's house we drove through the neighborhoods and I had never seen so many lights on houses and Christmas trees in the windows. I wondered what it would be like to live in a house that had a Christmas tree and presents under it. In school, the teachers always wanted you to share what gifts you got for Christmas. Wonder why they had to be so nosey. Don't they know some kids just don't get presents or have a birthday cake. I listened to the other kids, namin' off dolls, doll houses, and GI Joes. I had no idea what I was supposed to have gotten. The first year, the teacher asked me what I got. "nothing," I said. All the other kids laughed at me, so after that I lied. Seems I lied a lot, just so the other kids wouldn't laugh. I guess you learn early you are suppose to fit in, but somehow I was always on the outside lookin' in.

Joes, he tried to tell me, "Now, Little Anna, you knows you not suppose to lie. You be proud of who you are." I wondered how I was supposed to do that.

We got to my Momma's Momma's house and she had a Christmas tree with presents. I didn't notice or listen much to what the grownups talked about that night. I just sat next to that tree all night hoping one of the presents was for me. Theys wasn't.

nine

"Anna," Nurse Julie touches my shoulder. "Why don't you go to the hotel and get some sleep. I will call you if there are any changes with your mother."

"Thanks, Julie, but I am okay. I will walk down to the café to get some coffee." As I grab my sweater, I say," You have my cell number, right?"

Julie nods and lets out a long sigh. Nurse Julie has been Momma's nurse on and off for the last two years. I had learned a bit about Nurse Julie during our small conversations around Momma's bed. She was pretty, in a tomboy kind of way, sort of short with a slim build, and short blonde hair. She always asked about my three children and I always asked about her brother who is serving his fifth year in the army. Julie's mom had passed away when she was twelve in an automobile accident and she was currently dating, but not in a serious relationship.

As I walk down the quiet corridor, I let out a small laugh as I think about the roles that my Momma and I have taken on: she like a child now and me the caregiver. I try not to let the anger overtake my thoughts again, as I say a small prayer; the only thing that has gotten me through the last two years.

I find a table to sit while I sip my coffee. I didn't realize how exhausted I was. I think about my Momma as I look out the window watching the late November Illinois rain fall ever so steadily against the windows, determined to bring cooler weather with every drop. Years have come and gone, and with them, so many things I have not allowed myself to think about. It just seems a lifetime ago. Everything is so different than when I was a child. But with Momma's illness comes a new chapter and old memories refusing to stay stored in my memory bank, pushing and fighting their way to the present. My mind drifts back to my childhood, as it has seemed to do a lot lately.

ten

My family moved back to Alabama from Illinois almost a year after we had moved there. The move back was not unlike the move when we left. School had only been out a week and I managed to survive the winter and welcomed spring with open arms. We woke up one mornin' and found Momma packin'; only the personal items, so I packed up the same clothes I packed when we left Alabama along with Joes' book and note; hidin' it under my clothes in a brown paper bag. We left all the household items once again. The same country music playin', the same cigarette smoked filled car, no pee stops unless daddy said so and crackers with canned potted meat for all the meals with water to wash it all down. Only difference this time, Daddy seemed happy and Momma, well she just sat in the front seat with a blank look on her face.

I worried about Momma, as she seemed to change her mood on the turn of a dime ever since that scene by the pond under the tree. For some reason she always insisted on me knowin' her little secrets: other men. When she would go meet them she started takin' me with her. I am not sure why. I always had to sit in the car. She would chatter on and on about those other men and lie to Daddy about what she did that day sayin', "Ain't that right, Anna Marie?" I would just nod my head. I hated being a part of her lies, as much as I hated livin' in Illinois.

I was so glad to see the big crepe myrtle in full bloom at the end of my Grammy's drive. Grammy and I were not necessarily close, but yet I felt safe with her around and we seemed to have a connection. I loved the way she smelled, like her flower garden or if you could bottle sunshine and warmth, that would be my Grammy. I wondered if she would remember me. I was a whole year older. I wondered what it would be like to be back in Alabama without Joes livin' on the backside of the farm. Would Daddy be happier? Maybe I wouldn't get so many beatin's. I hoped the parties would not continue here like they did in Illinois. We pulled into the driveway. Daddy smiled as Grammy came toward him and she hugged him and said hi to Momma. Then she looked right at me and said, "Hi Anna Marie, I think you have gotten taller. Are you hungry?" I couldn't believe it; my Grammy looked right at me and wanted to know if I was hungry! I guess she wouldn't have any way to know my belly was always hungry.

I looked at Daddy to make sure I wasn't going to get in trouble; it seemed he always was takin' away the good things. But he just nodded at me as if to say it was okay. So I looked at my Grammy with a big smile and said, "Yes ma'am, my belly is hungry."

This was a great start to being back in Alabama. Grammy made us ham, eggs, grits, biscuits and red-eyed gravy. No one could cook like Grammy. I ate until my belly was about to pop. After the meal, I helped clean up the dishes as fast as I could, my mind was on gettin' back to Joes' place; I dashed outside and ran toward my favorite place in the whole world. On the way, I made a detour to pick up my stick that was still lyin' where I left it over a year ago. This was a great day. I walked slowly up to Joes place. Not knowing what to expect. It looked the same except Joes was gone. The pen where Bell and Star lived was empty. Grandpa had gotten rid of them after Joes died. Strut and the rest of the chickens were gone. Where Joes had his vegetable garden was now just a bed of weeds. Everythin' was the same like it was waitin' on Joes to return.

I let out a sigh and walked toward the front porch and saw the two pails hangin' on the nails where Joes had left them. I slowly walked up the stairs and sat down, thinkin' this was the safest place in the world. My heart was beatin' fast and my belly filled up with an ache so big it seemed to overtake my whole body. I looked out into Joes' yard; the trees had gotten bigger and the moss hangin' from them seemed to be as sad as the cicadas singin' in the background, almost like they missed Joes hummin'.

Rememberin' the stories of Joes and his smile, and his gentle hands tendin' my bruises. I stood up and walked to the door, my shakin' hand on the doorknob. I took a deep breath and walked inside.

I'd only been in here once, all the years I knew Joes. 'Cause Joes say it not proper for a little girl to be in a grown man's house. It smelled old, though I'm not really sure what old smells like, except Joes I guess. It was dusty, and my heart beat a little faster, like I had been runnin' in a race. It looked like Joes should be here; everythin' looked like he just took a walk and would be back later. It was only one room. A kitchen, if you can call it that, tucked in one corner. A wood burnin' cook stove, still had his kettle on it. A shelf over the cook stove, with two tin plates, two tin cups; from which we drank our sweet tea. Two forks, one big spoon, one iron skillet, a sink, no running water; Joes always carried his water from the well. A small table with one chair at it, a single size bed, no sheets, just a worn out mattress with a quilt on top, a single light bulb hangin' from the ceilin' and Joes' radio. No other furniture. The floor was made out of the same wood that the shack was made of. Everything was made of wood. The walls were the same inside as outside and the cracks in-between them brought in rays of sunshine. Yet it had a warm feelin' about it. Maybe all the love Joes carried inside him, somehow it settled into his home. The room had a fireplace with a mantel over it and wood stacked inside waitin' to be burned.

I let out a big sigh, missin' Joes so bad my heart hurt. Tears spilled out of my eyes onto my cheeks and ran down my dress, like the sky just opened up for its spring rain. I could not stop them from comin'. Funny thing about tears, they can mean so many things: sorrow, pain, or happiness. But I knew these tears were because Joes was not here and my world felt incomplete. He would have been so happy to see me. I could just hear him say to me, "Now, Little Anna, look how you dunna grow." And then he'd laugh under his breath, like he was afraid to laugh from the belly. I don't reckon I ever heard him laugh out loud. Oh Joes, I thought, my heart is empty. I guess Joes was the only happy memory in my life and when that was gone, well it's gone. And it leaves an empty space so big you get lost in it. I looked around and I saw a paper stickin' out of a book that was sittin' on the mantel. Wrinkled and torn at the edge, I pulled the paper out of the book, not understandin' exactly what it was. Somethin' about the 14th Amendment, which was ratified by the states grantin' African Americans citizenship. I tucked it inside my pocket. It was dated 1868. I knocked the book off the mantel and more papers fell out all yellowed and wrinkled. Papers with Joes name on it, no last name, just Joes first name. And my family's last name. I didn't understand what all this was, so I put them back inside the book, pullin' the paper out of my pocket placin' it with the other papers. As I did I saw another paper wedged inside the book. I slowly pulled it out and turn it over. It was a picture. I stood there with my mouth hangin' open.

eleven

"Code blue, code blue!" I hear the announcement over the hospital intercom. I check my phone making sure I did not miss a phone call from Nurse Julie. Hospitals have an eerie quietness about them at 11 p.m and when you hear a voice come over the intercom announcing code blue, it leaves you with a deep emptiness and I always hope the person is not alone like Joes was when he passed away.

I can't remember in the last two years when I have had a peaceful night's sleep. My eyes feel so heavy and my head begins to pound.

My phone rings and it is my daughter Victoria Ann.

I smile as I answer. "Hello Princess, how is school?" In between my drives back and forth from Illinois to Alabama to take care of my mother, I managed to get her all settled into her apartment and her first year of college.

"Mother, I don't understand boys," she said. I smile. I love her voice. I love that we are close; I listen as she fills me in on the last few days of her life, school, how girls can be so jealous of one another, boyfriend woes, work and life as a college student. "Oh yes mother, can you please make a deposit in my account? I am running short. I will do better next month, promise." And then she has to go because her boyfriend is calling. "Love you Mom. Sorry. Didn't realize the time! Gotta go. Love you."

I smile as we hang up. Victoria Ann has always been a night owl. It was no surprise that my phone rang this late and her voice was full of excitement and energy. The first time I held Victoria Ann in my arms, my heart filled with a love so unimaginable. I cried and laughed at the same time. The joy that filled every fiber in my being as she grabbed my finger, our gazed locked onto one another as if to say best friends for life. I promised her I would always take care of her and love her. No one would ever hurt her. Her brown eyes sparkled as if she understood what I had promised.

Now, she is in her first year of college.

As I make my way back to Momma's room, my heart is full after getting off the phone with Victoria Ann. The fatigue settles in once again as I lay my head against the window and look at Momma. I can't seem to close my eyes and I am thankful she is resting well this evening. I turn and look out the window.

"Daddy God, thank You, for Your love, for showing me how to love, even when I didn't think I could. You brought me to a place to honor my Momma. Even that seemed impossible. But once again You showed me anything is possible with You."

The nurse walks in to check on Momma and I realize I have not slept.

After the nurse leave, I walk back to the window and see the sun peaking over the horizon in all its glory, reminding me that God has given us another day. I look back at Momma still asleep and my thoughts go back to my relationship with her.

Momma moves as if she is in pain. I walk over and touch her hand and she settles down. I hold her hand a little longer and wonder once again, what did you think when you held me in your arms for the first time? Was there ever a moment when your heart melted when you looked at me or was your heart ever filled with so much joy that it spilled over from the love you felt for me? Oh Momma, did tears ever slip down your cheeks when you thought I was hurt or in need? If I could just hear you say, "Anna Marie, I love you." I think that longing in my heart would go away. Oh Momma, why couldn't we have had a relationship like Victoria Ann and I have; the closeness and the friendship the two of us have. All the late night chats while we looked at the latest fashion magazines while consuming salty snacks and the laughter that would erupt as she taught me how to text message. Or the long nights she cried after her boyfriend broke up with her. I would hold her until she fell asleep knowing the ache I felt for her was my heart breaking along with hers. I know when she is hurting before she ever calls. I know when she has joy when I see her face. I know when she is hiding something when I look in her eyes. I know when she is trying to surprise me. I know her.

Oh, Momma, you never knew me.

A tear slips down my cheek as I squeeze Momma's hand ever so lightly. My heart is bursting with pain and longing for what will never be and what could have been.

"I tried, Momma," I whisper as I let go of Momma's hand and walk back to the window, trying to keep the anger from surfacing as I recall the words Momma so harshly lashed at me and the failed attempts at trying to get close to her; longing for her approval and love.

I let my mind drift back to the picture of Joes.

twelve

Why, I wondered, did Joes not tell me he had a wife and little girl? I could tell it is Joes, even though he is younger in the picture. It was his smile and his hands. He looked so happy in this picture. The picture was dated 1896. How old was Joes? What happen to his family? Where did he come from?

More and more questions piled on top of one another; I felt my mind would explode if I didn't get answers. I needed to talk to my Grammy. A noise startled me. I carefully put Joe's book back on the shelf. I heard it again. It sounded like somethin' was hittin' the side of the house. I heard my brother yellin' for me.

"dang!" I yelled. He never came back here. Why now I wondered?

I heard him callin' my name again, tellin' me he would tell Daddy if I didn't come out of Joes' house.

"I know you are in there crazy girl. You are not suppose to be in a colored man house!" He was yellin' as he threw another rock and hit the side of the house.

"what on earth do you want?" I yelled back. "and it is not a colored man's house, it is joe's house and he is in heaven with jesus".

"Daddy is lookin' for you!" he yelled.

I slowly opened the door to Joes' house and made my way to the porch steps and stood on them with my hands on my hips like I was protectin' Joes and his house. I looked at my brother standin' at the bottom of the stairs. He was taller than me. He turned 15 while we were in Illinois. As I stared at his brown hair and brown eyes, I realize he does not look like my Daddy at all. And I wondered why I never noticed that before.

"You are goin' to get a beaten' for bein' back here. What are you doing here anyways?" He asked.

"none of your business." I said. I ducked as the rock he threw came so close to my ear I could feel the heat off of it. "why do you have to be so darn mean? why can't you just be nice? does everyone in this family have to have a mean spot in them?"

He reached up and grabbed my arm, pullin' me down to the ground and kicked me in the side.

"Don't back talk to me crazy girl. Is this where you come to all day? You think you can hide from me?" He was kickin' me on the legs and in the back with every word he spoke. I began to crawl away, but he dragged me back toward him. "You can either take a beaten' from me or I can tell Daddy you were back here. You can pick." He laughed. I managed to get up and began to run, forgettin' my stick. I headed straight toward Grammy's house, hopin' I would outrun him.

Summer was not yet here, but the sand was already hot as it burned my feet. The blisters on my toes from where my brother held a cigarette lighter to them a few nights before we left Illinois were beggin' for me to just stop runnin', but I knew I couldn't for fear the "thing" would happen. Sweat began to drip down my forehead. I ran faster and faster, lookin' back to see how close he was, only to run straight into an anthill. It took no time for those ants to cover my body; I had to stop runnin' and began to swipe them off as fast as I could. I was so mad at myself. Why did the ants have to build right in the middle of the road and why did I not notice it coming to Joes? My brother caught up with me and instead of helpin' me, he dragged me back to the anthill and held me down while the ants cover my legs and began to leave dozens of red bites. I wondered at that moment if they were bitin' me because they were scared or because they were angry that I ran into their hill. I decided they were angry that I messed up their house.

I finally kicked my way free from my brother's grip and rolled out of the anthill. He stood up and gave one final kick to my legs and walked away, "Stupid girl," he murmured. I was thankful the 'thing" did not happen. It seemed to be happening less and less.

I guess he became bored. I was thankful he lost interest in me as I sat there and examined my bites. They started swellin' like balloons being filled with water. I swear if I got the chance I was gonna run away. There had to be a family who wanted me. I could hear my Daddy callin' for us, so I picked myself up and ran back to Joes to get my stick. For a moment, I wanted to go back into Joes' house and take the book and the picture with me so I could show Grammy and have her tell me what she knew about Joes and his family, but instead I turned and headed toward her house, hopin' to come back soon.

Taking in the surroundin's, in spite of my brother ruinin' my peaceful moments at Joes' house, I was happy to be back in Alabama. I never thought I would say that. All my life I wanted to run away from this place, but I found a place I hated more, and people I trusted even less.

As I made my way back to Grammy's house, I felt the warmth of the sun beamin' down on my face, remindin' me that summer was well on its way. The sand under my feet was warm but cool as my toes dug under the surface. I took in the smell of the pine, and from somewhere out of sight, hidden behind the pine trees and undergrowth, the scent of honeysuckle made it's way to tickle my nose. Yes, it was good to be back, close to Joes' house, close to my Grammy's. I knew I never got a hug from her and of course Joes is gone to be in heaven, but this was where I felt the safest in the world. I realized bad things happen to you, I guess no matter where you are at, or where you live, or where you feel safe, or where you are scared. But when those things happen, this was where I wanted to be. I cannot explain it, some things I guess don't need an explanation.

As I came closer to Grammy's house, I could feel a change coming. I was not sure if it was good or bad, but once when I told Joes I didn't like change and I asked why do things have to change, Joes said to me, "Little Anna, don't be afraid of change, cause with change comes the chance for yous to grow." Joes, he was always sayin' things I didn't understand but I liked his words anyway.

My Daddy was standin' at the end of the driveway looking at me as I walked toward him. I knew I was in trouble, hopin' he would not notice the swollen red dots that by now actually looked like I had a really bad sunburn. Oh, how I didn't want to explain how I got them or where I was at when the ants decided to take out all their fury on my legs, but no such luck. Daddy was already takin' off his belt, grabbin' my arm and swingin' me around so he could begin the beatin'.

"You are not going to start disappearin' like you did before. You are forbidden to leave this house. Do you understand me?"

"yes sir," I said between cryin', hopin' he would stop. But he kept goin' until my Grammy came out and said that was enough.

My Daddy stopped, looked at me, and ordered me to go stand in the corner with my nose pressed into it. I could hear my Grammy and Daddy talkin', but could not understand what they were sayin'. So, I stood there in the corner feelin' dizzy and sick, not sure if it was from the beatin' or the bites. I must have dozed off, for the next thing I knew my Grammy came to check on my ant bites. I don't know how long I stayed there, but pretty sure I had missed dinner and supper. She did not say a word as she put ointment on them and sighed as she touched the new bruises that were makin' their appearances from the beatin'. She announced, like she was talkin' to herself rather than to me, that I was runnin' a fever and gave me something for it. Her hands were small and strong, not like Joes whose hands were big and strong, but gentle. I wished Joes was here. Tears came to my eyes again rememberin' him and I looked at my Grammy and took a deep breath getting up the nerve to ask about Joes.

"grammy?" I barely whispered. "did you know joes?"

She looked up at me; her eyes were a light blue like you could see through them, and her hair red, but not a bright red, it looked old like her with gray lines in it.

"Anna Marie, Joe took care of your bruises didn't he?"

I held my breath. How did she know? Joes said I could never say his name. I never did. How would she know this? I let out a long sigh and answered, "yes ma'am."

My Grammy didn't say anythin' for a long time, like she was thinkin' about somethin' but then she said, "Anna Marie, we cannot talk about Joe, do you understand?"

I nodded, disappointed that I could not ask all the questions I had about the picture and the papers I had found in Joe's house.

If I were not feeling so tired, hungry, and sick, I would have protested but I did not have the strength. I did get the feelin' she wanted to talk about him, so decided I would make a point to ask her again.

"Anna Marie, you have to stay here in the corner, your Daddy is determined. But I will bring you some food."

My feet hurt from the cigarette lighter burns, my ant bites were stingin', and my tummy was needin' some food. I am not sure how long Grammy was gone, but I had fallen asleep standin' in that corner with my nose pressed into it. The last thing I remember was smellin' the lemon cleaner that Grammy used to clean her wooden walls, wishin' I had not missed supper. That was the first day we were back in Alabama. The rest of the summer, Grammy found a way for me to avoid Daddy's beatin'. I will forever be grateful for that summer, well parts of it anyway.

thirteen

I walk back to Momma's room, hoping she is still asleep. I look down at her and see this elderly woman with salt and pepper hair, more salt than pepper. I can't help but wonder what her childhood was like. I had never thought about that as a child. All I wanted was her love and protection. Now as I look at her lying in this bed fighting for her life, my heart lurches into this insurmountable pain. It is mixed with pity, sadness, and anger, and a hole so big a person could get overtaken by it. I have to shake it off and focus on what the next step of taking care of her would be. At this point I could not let all these emotions overtake the logic of why I was here. I begin to feel the urgency to get home. I miss the boys and I have a business to run. I have this endless guilt of needing to be home when I am here taking care of her. Yet, I had asked God two years ago, *"Do You want me here? Taking care of a person, who all my life but abandoned me, ignored me, and told me she didn't even like me. She didn't protect me."*

God answered.

My mind drifts back to the summer I lived with my Grammy.

fourteen

The end of summer was drawin' near. School was startin' in two weeks. I had spent the summer helpin' Grammy with the food cannin' and a neighbor with his tobacco harvestin'. I didn't mind helpin' Grammy. It kept me out of Momma's way and my brothers would not mess with me as long as I was with her. That, and I ended up givin' them the money I made in the tobacco field just so they would leave me alone. I would walk down to Grammy's house before six in the mornin'. There, she would have breakfast waitin' for me. That is when Grammy let me have my first cup of strong, black Folgers coffee. I became a coffee addict after that summer.

We would begin our chores after Grammy put on her gloves a big straw hat and for some reason an apron. She looked so small and frail. I really liked her. I guess she is the second person I have ever liked. We spent endless hours shellin' butter beans, pullin' peanuts out of the scorchin' hot sandy mounds, gratin' corn off the cob to freeze for cream corn later in the year, cannin' tomatoes, and long hours of slow cookin' cane juice into the sweetness of cane syrup, which I delighted in when Grammy made homemade biscuits.

After I was finished with my day, I would always take the long way home, back by Joes' place and sit on his front porch and tell him about my day. I guess most people would think I was crazy for talkin' to someone who was in heaven, but I just knew Joes could hear me. I kept lookin' at his picture and the papers I had found. I still had questions I did not have answers to. Grammy and I never talked about Joes again that summer. Every time I would try to bring it up, she would look at me and shake her head. The attempt would leave me frustrated and wonderin' if I would ever get my answers. I didn't need conversation, just answers and Grammy was the key to all of them. As I worked with her in her flower gardens, it was easy to let my mind wander. I could think about anythin' I wanted to and no one could take that away; not my rotten mean brothers nor my Dads "look" that meant I was gettin' the belt. No, my mind was my refuge which always landed on runnin' away and findin' a family that loved me. That and Joes. I always dreaded going home. I could just live right here in Joes place, or anywhere really, as long as it was not with Momma and Daddy. As I closed the front door, leavin' the comfort of being around Joes' house, I let out a big sigh and headed home.

The next mornin' was my last day to finish up with the tobacco harvest. We pulled the dry tobacco leaves off the sticks and wrapped them in burlap bags, ready to be carried off to the auction. I loved the smell of dry tobacco leaves, earthy and sweet at the same time. It did not smell like cigarettes at all. In fact cigarettes ruins the beauty of the tobacco smell. It reminded me of grandpa's pipe. He always left it on the mantel after he finished smokin' it. I would sneak into the t.v. room and suck on it. I loved the way it tasted.

The neighbor handed out the last of my pay, and I looked at it as I longed to buy new school clothes and maybe more than one pair of shoes. But as I walked home, I knew my brothers would be waitin' to take it from me. Darn brothers. I turned the corner and there they were hands out with smirks on their faces. "You better find a way to keep it comin' or else,"while making a fist at me. It didn't seem fair I worked all summer, and because they were the bullies, they got to keep my money. Wouldn't do no good to tell Momma and Daddy, since they weren't ever home anymore. I wasn't sure what they did, but was thankful we all seemed to have gone our own ways this summer.

Close to school startin', the kids were excited because Momma and Daddy were goin' to take us school shoppin'. I was not sure why since they always end up fightin'. They never agreed on dresses or pants for us girls. My brothers were goin' on about tie-dye somethin' or another, my oldest sister was sayin' something about bell bottoms jeans. I just tuned everyone out, hopin' that this year I would find a friend who would play with me.

We got to the store and I was lookin' around. Daddy came up to me and said I had to pay for my own clothes this year since I made money in the tobacco field. I looked up at him dreadin' to lie but had no choice to avoid a beatin' from my brothers. Hoping Daddy would feel sorry for me, "i lost it," I said.

"You lost it, dangit girl, how stupid can you be? Well, you will not get anythin' this year. You better hope your shoes from last year fit. Lost it!? I know you cannot be my kid. I couldn't have created one this stupid." His boot landed on my backside. I held in my tears and shame as a young girl watched while Daddy grabbed my arm shakin' me and callin' me stupid.

Momma came over, "What have you done now to upset your Daddy, Anna Marie? I swear child, we cannot take you anywhere. You are always embarrassin' us. Let go of her arm before you draw attention to us, honey." She looked at Daddy. I guess that was the closest Momma ever came close to protecting me.

"This dumb girl lost her money, so she gets nothin' new for school."

"Oh for heaven's sake, Anna Marie, you do bring on so much trouble for yourself. You are the most awkward, troublesome child I have ever seen." Momma said as she rolled her eyes in frustration.

I looked at Momma hopin' she would know that my brothers took my money. Hopin' that for once she would stand up for me, but she did neither. She went about pickin' out dresses for the younger girls and my brothers watchin' the whole thing with a smirk on their face, as they got the tie-dyed shirts they wanted and my oldest sister got her bell bottom jeans and everyone but me got new shoes. And just like that, my school year started with worn out clothes and shoes that were too small.

The end of August Momma and Daddy got jobs in the local factory. Our world was about to change forever.

fifteen

Daddy was mad about somethin' again. I could hear him and Momma fightin'. He stormed into the room where we were doin' our homework and yelled at us to go to bed. I wanted to protest. We had not had dinner, or a bath, and my homework was not finished. But Daddy's anger was different tonight, so I got up along with the other children and we went to bed. It was only 6:30 and still daylight outside. How was a child supposed to sleep when the sky was still bright? All eight of us kids were in the same bedroom: my brothers, Mike and Jack were in a corner on their own pallet, my oldest sister Nell, and the youngest sister, Diane and Molly were on one and Shelly, Frannie, and I were on the same pallet closest to the door. We were all tryin' to hear what the big fight was about that led to our early bedtime without supper. They were talkin' about another couple, someone they had met at the factory. Momma wanted another party and Daddy was against it. Why, Momma, do you want these parties? Rememberin' the parties in Illinois, I squeezed my eyes shut and tried not to hear, hoping Daddy would win this fight. We laid there for what seemed a lifetime. The fightin' finally stopped and we all fell asleep only to be waken by Daddy runnin' around the room trying to wake all of us up. He yelled each name, picked up Diane the baby sister, and put her under his arm like she was a football as he was screamin' for us to hold hands. He led us out of the smoked filled room. The house was engulfed in fire.

Momma was already outside in the car cryin'. At first I thought she was cryin' for us, but she kept yellin' at my Daddy to go back inside the house to get her weddin' band she had put on the night stand. He ran around to the side porch and disappeared into the smoke and the house that was now ablaze with fire. I wondered why he would risk his life for a piece of gold to go around Momma's finger when all they did was fight. I held my breath waitin' for him to come out. Momma was cryin' and the other kids were talkin' endlessly. I think because they were scared. It was like watchin' Daddy in slow motion as he came out of the fire covered in black smoke.

Momma was askin' him over and over, "Did you get the ring? Did you get the ring?" I thought it odd that she did not ask Daddy if he was okay, because I was wonderin' if he was. He looked as black as Joes. He sat in the front seat and put his head on the steerin' wheel and handed Momma her ring. She took it and started talking' about how they wouldn't be able to replace that ring and how good it was that Daddy had gone back to get it. Momma never did ask Daddy if he was okay. She never asked any of us kids if we were okay. She just sat in the front seat as we drove to Grammy's, with what look like a small grin on her face. What would my Momma have to be smilin' about? We just lost all our clothes and shoes. I didn't much care since my shoes were too small anyway, but they were all I had and I wasn't too sure that Daddy would buy us anymore; since he had the rule about one pair a year. I hadn't finish my homework. I wondered if we would go to school tomorrow.

Daddy turned the headlights off as we pulled very slowly into Grammy's driveway. We parked, but Daddy did not get out. He said in a very quiet, low voice we would sleep in the car until mornin'. He didn't want to wake Grammy and Grandpa. I didn't think I had ever heard my Daddy's voice sound like it was so far away. The words he spoke did not match the look in his eyes or the sound of his voice. I wondered what he was really thinkin'. You never know what is in a person's head. Just like my thoughts of runnin' away and findin' a family that loves me. No one knows my thoughts, except when I shared them out loud with Joes.

As we found a comfortable position to sleep, I could smell the smoke on Daddy. It smelled like dark, wet charcoal mixed with some kind of chemical. I could see Daddy's profile. He just sat there starin' at nothin'. His eyes looked empty and Momma she just sat there with the same look on her face. I wondered what they were really thinkin', as I nodded off to sleep. I was thankful we all got out alive, even my rotten brothers. As my eyes began to slowly close they popped wide open as I realized I lost Joes black book and note in the fire. My belly began to churn and my eyes filled with tears that would not stay behind my eyelids. I felt like I had lost Joes all over again. The hole in my heart got even bigger. I had been takin' Joes' black book out every day and tryin' to read it even though I did not understand it. It always made me feel close to the only person I have ever loved and the only person who had ever told me I was special.

"joes?" I whispered. "can you hear me? i am so sorry joes. i am so sorry." As my eyes got heavy with sleep, I swore I heard Joes say, "Little Anna, I am here and it is okay."

My eyes felt swollen and heavy as I woke up to Daddy closin' the car door. I watched Daddy walkin' up to Grammy's front door. The look he had on his face was gone and now he looked normal. Grammy came to the door and I reckon he told her what happen. She hugged him for a long time. As I watched this exchange, I wondered why Daddy didn't hug us. It couldn't be because he doesn't know how.

People heard about our loss and brought us bags full of clothes and shoes. For the first time, I had more than one pair of shoes to wear to school, but the hole in my heart kept me from bein' happy about that. As the school year came and went I found myself likin' Grammy's house: no beatin's, no fightin' between Momma and Daddy, no dirty water to take baths in, and no missed meals. I was even allowed to watch Julia Childs on t.v. after school. I am not sure how I got this privilege, but I was thankful. I loved her voice and the fancy foods she made. I wanted to be like her when I grew up. I wanted to have fancy dishes and table cloths, and friends to laugh with as we ate our fancy food.

Normally, the only time we were ever allowed to watch t.v. was when Daddy watched his westerns and then you were afraid to breathe because he would get mad if you even shifted your position. Once you sat on the floor, you stayed in that position until the show was over. You learned to sit where your legs would not go to sleep. But at Grammy's I sat on the sofa and usually got the t.v. room all to myself because the other kids didn't like the cookin' show. Yes, life was pretty good for this girl, but just as quick as it was given, it was taken away.

Daddy came home and announced he had found a place for us to move. My heart sank right down to the bottom of my feet. Momma, she was so happy, she did not like my Grammy or livin' in my Grammy's house. I would hear her talkin' to my Daddy in a low voice about him findin' us our own place. "I am dyin' here." I would hear her say to him. I didn't want to leave Grammy's house, but I had no say. We packed up our clothes and moved into the house that would end my Momma and Daddy's marriage. Our troubled lives would take a downward spiral, that even I could not imagine.

At our new house, Frannie and I were sittin' outside and we heard Momma and Daddy yellin's at each other. The bedroom window was open and we just looked at each other and sighed.

I said to Frannie, "i ain't gonna sit here and listen to this fight. wanna go down to the pond and hide?"

Frannie shook her head and said, "Annie, you know I don't like to be around the pond."

"i know." I said as I got up and walked towards the pond by myself.

I thought about the day we snuck off to the pond and Frannie fell in. I thought she was goin' to drown. But I jumped in and we managed to kicks our way back to the shallow end. Frannie, she don't go to the pond anymore. I was at the pond most of the day until I saw Frannie standin' in the distance wavin' for me to come home.

I ran to meet her and she looked like she had been cryin'.

"frannie, what has you all snotted up?" I said to her.

"Oh Annie, I heard Momma and Daddy talkin's about the house fire. Annie, they started it and was goin' to leave us in the house."

"frannie, now stop your snottin' and tell me exactly what you heard."

I listened to Frannie, and the hole in my heart just got bigger. I found myself once again wondering if Joes' Jesus was real? I couldn't understand how a Momma and Daddy could ever think about leavin' their kids in a burnin' house. I guess I should be thankful my Daddy decided to save us.

My life made no sense. I sighed so big I felt all my air leave my body. What was my purpose? Why was I born? A kid should never have to live this way. I wish I could ask Joes. He always had somethin' smart to say even if I didn't understand it. I remember him tellin' me not to be afraid of change, it makes you grow. I guess I almost missed my chance to grow.

sixteen

"Momma," I whisper, "It is okay. I am here. Everything is going to be okay. The doctor is on his way. Can you try to take a deep breath? Just try Momma." She is gasping for air as I wrap my arms gently around her shoulders, holding her up, wanting her to feel my love for her. I ring for the nurse, and I know it only takes seconds for them to get to the room, but it seems like an eternity.

As the doctor and nurses begin to work on Momma, I step out of the room to say a quiet prayer. The doctor joins me a few minutes later. He looks at me with empathy, "Anna, we can't do anything more for your mother. You told me her wishes were to die in her home, is that correct?"

"Yes," I whisper.

"We will make arrangements with Hospice and send her home tomorrow."

"Okay," I manage to say as I am thinking about all the preparations that need to be taken care of. I call Molly, Frannie, and Diane to tell them that it is time to take her home and for them to call the other kids. I go back inside Momma's room after my phone call; she lies on the bed, frail and pale.

"Momma," I say, "I am going to meet Molly and Diane downstairs and then I am going to run some errands. I will be back in a few hours. Will you be okay until then? You won't give the girls a hard time will you?"

As I smile at her, she manages to give me a faint smile back. I kiss her on the forehead and close the door behind me. She has already fallen asleep. I don't want Momma's house to feel like it is the end for her. I want it peaceful and beautiful. Hospice would deliver a bed, but I wanted her to have new bedding in her favorite shades of purple. So I go shopping and bring her new bedding home and wash it, waiting for Hospice to bring the bed. I clean her tiny apartment while thinking how sad it is to end up in a place like this.

Momma was diagnosed with ovarian cancer 2 years and 4 months ago. I sit down in Momma's tiny living room and as I look around at the meager furniture, the television set, and her old white tennis shoes by the front door, I burst into an uncontrollable, gut wrenching cry. I know I am crying for the things that were not, the things that could have been, and for all of the things that happened. Why God? Why did it have to be this way? The tears would not stop as I cry myself into exhaustion and fall asleep, only to be awakened by the doorbell. Hospice is here to set up Momma's bed. The last part of the journey with my Momma is about to take place. My mind begins to drift back to my childhood once again.

seventeen

That fall, Momma and Daddy got a divorce. Momma, she moved in with a man that was mean. He had four daughters and one son. I didn't like any of them. And Daddy moved in with a woman who had a daughter. They didn't get married, just lived with one another. People in town talked about them cause I would be hearin' what the kids at school would be sayin' about us. "Shameful," was what they'd say. "Just shameful that they be shackin' up." I didn't know much about grown up talk, but I did understand Momma and Daddy should not be shackin' up.

My oldest sister, Nell, she ran off and got married just before she turned 18. My oldest brother, Jack, who was 16, just up and left home to live in Florida. He said Momma and Daddy didn't care about us anyways. My youngest brother, Mike, who was 15, he ran away the followin' spring to North Carolina. He left a note for my Momma sayin' he wasn't takin' this crap no more. Momma's new boyfriend beat on him and beat him really bad one day when my brother tried to stop him from beatin' on Momma. Frannie, Diane, Molly, Shelly and I spent time with Momma most of the time and Daddy sometimes.

Then one day, Daddy he just shows up and says we've got to live with him. And just like that Momma packed our bags and we moved in with him and his girlfriend. Everythin' was upside down again. Life just seemed so confusin' to me. Everythin' seemed so temporary. I didn't feel like livin' with Momma or livin' with Daddy. I once overheard his girlfriend say, "I gave my daughter up to be with you, why do we have to have your brats here?" Her daughter would come visit them. Daddy's girlfriend seemed to like her daughter and they laughed and seemed to have a good time when she was here for her visits. I didn't understand why her Momma gave her up. My Daddy just looked at her and walked away. I wish he had just kept walkin' and took us with him.

But Daddy insisted we live with him and she would have to deal with it. We moved three towns away from where I grew up. Daddy's new girlfriend did not want him runnin' into my Momma. Our lives did not get any better with this new arrangement. Daddy's new girlfriend acted like we were her personal servants by always makin' us wait on her when Daddy wassn't around. Barkin' orders for us to make her tea, bring her lunch, clean the house, start dinner and make supper. I would just tune her out. I kept doin' my chores all the while hummin'. She told me to stop but I kept hummin'. She stomped out of the room like she was a five year old. I would smile. She couldn't take away my hummin' or my thoughts.

Frannie and I went to visit Momma on a rainy Saturday. Daddy dropped us off at the end of the road leadin' up to Momma's and her new boyfriend's house. Daddy did not like Momma's new boyfriend either, but I wondered if he dropped us off because Momma's new boyfriend had threatened to kill my Daddy if he ever saw him again. We walked slowly not mindin' that we were drippin' wet from the rain. Neither one of us wanted to go. Momma's new boyfriend was mean. I think he was the meanest person I had ever met in my life. He was always beatin' his kids, not with a belt like Daddy did me, but with his fist. There was no peace in that house at all. The winter before when we went to visit we sat in the car, part of the time just to keep warm. Because he wouldn't let the gas company fill the tank to warm the house. Momma she would sit there, smoke her cigarettes, and listen to her country music on her eight track tapes, with bruises on her face from where he would beat her. I wondered if she ever thought about leavin' him.

As we approached the house we could hear the yellin' and fightin'. We did not want to go in, but knew we had too. We opened the door and went to the back of the house where the kitchen was. We could hear Momma's boyfriend yellin' and cussin'. As we approached the kitchen door, we heard a gunshot. We froze, and for a moment dead silence, then we heard our Momma cryin'. We ran into the kitchen to see her on the floor with her boyfriend sittin' on top of her holdin' the gun to her head. Frannie and I screamed at the same time. He looked up and pointed the gun at us, yellin' for us to leave the room. Momma was cryin' tellin' us to do what he said. I looked at her and I could see her face was a bloody mess. His daughter was standin' next to him with a bloody lip. Frannie and I ran out the front door and hid under the porch, cryin'. We did not want him to kill her. Frannie and I held each other and I started talkin' to Joes as fast as I could.

"joes, can you hear me? please joes tell your jesus don't let that man kills our momma. you said he gives us what we wants. i don't wants her dead, joes. i will do whatever he wants me to. tell him joes. joes, i have frannie here with me. joes, she is really scared. please joes." I squeezed my eyes shut and cried.

"Annie, who's you talkin' to?" Frannie whispered, "Ain't nobody here but you and me?"

"shh, frannie i am tryin' to hear joes."

I don't know how long we were under the porch when I heard Momma sayin', "Girls, where are you?" We came out from under the porch. Frannie and I looked at each others and let out a long sigh. It felt like I hadn't breathed in a long time. We were thankful she was alive. Momma's eyes were almost swollen shut and her lip was as big as an egg.

"momma," I said as I reached to touch her face, "come home with us. frannie and i will take care of your face for you." Momma moved her face from my hand and stood up, pullin' us with her and told us we had to go to bed. Frannie and I could hardly sleep. We overheard the mean man's daughters talkin' about hatin' our Momma and wished she would move out. They say it her fault theys daddy got mad. I wanted my Momma to leave but didn't know where she would go. I had a restless night sleep and was thankful when I saw the sun comin' up. That meant Frannie and I could leave right after breakfast.

As Frannie and I walked to the end of the road waitin' for Daddy I began to think about the people in my life. What was wrong with them anyways? There had to be more to life than fightin' and so much hate and anger. I made myself a promise that night; no man would ever have a chance to hit me twice. That was a promise I intended to keep.

Daddy picked us up and we decided not to tell him what happened. He never asked how our visits with Momma went. 'Sides his girlfriend was always with him. He wouldn't dare bring up anythin' about Momma in front of her.

Frannie and I lay in bed that night. My Daddy provided us a real bed. For the first time in our lives, we did not sleep on a pallet. As we talked, we dreamed of a different family and what we would be when we grew up. Frannie wanted to be a nurse and I wanted to be a lawyer. We would whisper about a different life into the early mornin' hours, makin' a promise that our kids would be loved. We wouldn't let each other date mean men and that we would remain best friends. We always ended our talks with a pinky promise.

As the months passed, Daddy seemed to change. I ain't quite sure I could put my finger on it, but he was changin'. He seemed sad and not as mean. I would take that for now.

School was not much better; as I got older I realized just how different my family life was from most of the other kids at school. I never had a friend in school. Frannie and I stayed close to one another while at school; we were all the other one had.

The followin' summer, Frannie and I had to get jobs. My Daddy's girlfriend didn't want Daddy to spend money on us for anythin'. Frannie and I had to start payin' for everythin' we needed. So we got jobs bussin' tables in a local restaurant. I didn't mind. We had our very first taste of soda drinks. I tasted butter on a biscuit for the first time and even had the chance to taste milk, which I did not like. But my favorite was ice cream on blackberry cobbler. We had never had ice cream. It had to be the best thing I had ever put in my mouth. I thought about Joes when I tried all the new things to eat and wondered if he had ever tasted butter, milk, and ice cream. Frannie did not like being out front, so she washed dishes. I, on the other hand, loved bein' out front. Strangers who did not know me seemed to like me. They would chat with me and asked me questions about what I liked to do; asking if I was a cheerleader in school? They didn't know I was not popular and that the other kids did not notice me, but I loved the attention. They didn't seem to think that I was any different than any other young teenage girl. I think this was the first time and the first place that I felt "normal." I would walk into that restaurant with my head held high. I think I even walked differently. I worked hard and before I knew it the owner promoted me to run the cash register with a raise.

He said to me, "Anna Marie, if you keep learnin' about how a restaurant is run, you might just be a manager someday." I knew most of our regular customers by name and knew what they would order on what day, and would place the order before they had to ask. The waitress would go up to the table to take their order and they would say, "Anna Marie already knows," and give me a wink. They were like my family. I loved everythin' about the restaurant business. I would come in early and watch Tizzy the cook; the way she ordered the food and planned the meals. Once she let me help plan the meals for the weekend. That is when she tried new menu ideas to see if they would work their way into the weekday rotation. "Anna Marie," she would say, "always be creative with your weekend meals. Give the customers things to eat they would not think to cook. Dream. Nothin' holdin' you back but yourself. I know you dream girl, I catch you sometimes with that far away look in your eyes." She laughed. "What do you dream about anyways?"

"oh i don't know tizzy, a little of this and a little of that," I would reply. She would just shake her head and smile. I could never let her inside my head to know my thoughts. That was a special place. Only person I ever let in was Joes.

Down the street from where I worked was a little dress shop. I had been lookin' at a sweater in the window for weeks. They had it displayed with a pair of jeans. I had never owned a sweater or a pair of jeans before. The sweater was dark blue with white zigzags on it. I now could afford to buy it along with the jeans for school. I was so excited to go shoppin'. Frannie and I giggled and chattered all the way home about how different we were goin' to look this year for school. We had to get permission from Daddy to walk back into town to do our shoppin'. When we got home, Daddy was not there but his girlfriend was, so we asked her if we could go shoppin'.

"You will have to ask your Daddy when he gets home," she said.

"when will he be home?" I asked.

"What are you wantin' to shop for?"

"as you know, frannie and i have worked all summer and we wants to go school clothes shoppin'."

She just looked at us and asked how much money we had made this summer.

"$500.00," I replied.

"Well, you know you owe me half of the money for watchin' your snotty little sisters all summer so you could work." She grinned at me almost darin' me to defy her. I could feel my cheeks gettin' red and my heart started beatin' faster as I looked at her with my mouth wide open and told her in no uncertain words how much I disliked her and there was no way she would take our money that we worked hard for all summer. Her hand landed on my face with enough force that it sent me stumblin' backwards. Frannie reached out and grabbed me by the arm. I was stunned and could not believe she had just slapped me.

"You disrespectful little witch. I will see to it that you go live in an orphanage! The whole lot of you brats."

I looked at her and smiled and said, "any place would be better than with you." I was determined she would not get the better of me. Did she really think I cared if I lived with her or not? An orphanage sounded better to me every day. Molly, Frannie, Diane, and I went into the bedroom and shut the door. She was yellin' at us to come out and do the list of chores she had for us. I told her no. I could just see her face turnin' a bright red as it often did when she would get upset. She was short and very robust. She had short black hair and was not attractive at all. She was furious with me and said I would get it when Daddy got home. I was sure she was right. I smiled as she kept screamin' at me through the locked door and thought the beatin' would be worth it this time. I remembered Joes' words about gettin' along with people and respectin' them like you wanted to be respected, but somehow I could not bring myself to respect a woman who let me know every day how much she really hated me. I told her once, that it did not bother me that she hated me, because there was no love lost. I was not really sure what that meant. I had overheard a girl say it to boy at school, but by the reaction I got from Daddy's girlfriend it must be bad.

It was not that I did not try to like her, I really tried, but she would talk bad about my Momma and Grammy, and she was not nice to us when Daddy wasn't around. Once when Daddy was at work she would not let us have food or drink the entire day while she had us pullin' weeds from around the fence. It was hot and we all had bad sunburns. Diane's even bubbled up on her poor arms. So I quit botherin' myself about it and just let it be what it was. Sometimes you just wait things out until they change, because change always came.

Daddy came home from work and ordered Frannie and I out of the bedroom. Belt in hand, he began my beatin', and true to Daddy being himself, it was a bad beatin'. Afterward I had to get the money I had earned all summer and hand it over to Daddy's girlfriend. My dream of jeans and the blue sweater was gone. She smirked at me as if to say I told you so. I don't think I have ever hated someone as much as I hated her right at that moment.

I had to make supper and sit in the kitchen on the floor while the family ate. Of course I didn't get supper that night. After they ate, I cleaned the kitchen, mopped, took out the trash, and on my way back into the house, Daddy ordered that I make him coffee. After the coffee had percolated, I poured him a cup and took it outside to him where he had been sittin' on the porch drinkin' beer. I hated the smell of beer about as much as I hated when he drank from the bottle. He tasted the coffee, and then ordered me to bring him the pot and as I stood in front of him he took the lid off and threw the entire pot in my face. I screamed, as hot liquid ran down my face onto my dress that stuck to me like hot glue. He kicked me in the stomach and told me I made his life miserable and he was takin' me to live with my Grammy and the other girls were goin' to live with my Momma. "Your Momma don't want you either. Maybe your Grammy will tolerate you for awhile." As I struggled to stand up straight I didn't think I had ever been so miserable and overjoyed at the same time. He stumbled to stand up, grabbing ahold of the post so he wouldn't fall. Drunk, he was as drunk as I had ever seen him. I hoped I never had to see him again, but was sad that Frannie, Molly, Shelly, Diane, and I would be separated.

Daddy and his girlfriend dropped me off at Grammy's house and left, without sayin' a word. I rang Grammy's doorbell and waited for her to answer the door.

"hi grammy," I smiled. "did daddy tell you he was dropping me off?" I stood there with a coffee stained dress and a face red with blisters. I knew I must have looked a mess.

"Anna Marie, what in the world happened to your face?"

"daddy threw a pot of coffee at it."

"Oh, Anna Marie, I know you think he is mean, but you know your Daddy loves you, right?"

I gave her a faint smile. I guess I had not figured out about love, but if Daddy's beatin's and his meanness was love, I think I could do without it. Grammy put some ointment on my face and neck that took the burn away. It took weeks for it to heal. I wondered if I would have scarrin' but it seemed Grammy's ointment was a miracle worker.

eighteen

I settled into a routine with my Grammy and Grandpa. I would feed the chickens and help Grammy in her flower garden, and of course I got in on the end of summer cannin' and freezin'. Which I did not mind since Grammy gave me a little money to buy a few outfits for school. On the first day back at Grammy's I went to Joes' place. I searched for my stick but it was gone, so I walked the sandy road for the first time since I could remember without it, hopin' I would not come across a snake. I saw an ant hill and remembered the summer my brother held me down so the ants would cover my legs. I didn't miss him. As I approached Joes' place I saw the vines were over takin' the front of the house and the front porch was saggin'. It no longer could carry the weight of the roof. It seemed to have given up its strength and given into its age. The tin roof was rusted and half of it was gone. I wondered how old this shack was. I crawled in a window for fear if I walked on the porch, the roof would continue to fall in. Everythin' was the same, just like it was when I left. I went to the mantel to get the book that had Joe's picture and papers in it, but the papers were gone. Why would someone leave the book and take the papers? Who would have taken the papers? Why? Everythin' else was in place just like Joes left it all those years ago.

"Joes," I said to an empty room, "I miss you everyday. I have had so much that has happened in my life, Joes. Momma and Daddy got a divorce and I am livin' with Grammy now. I am growin' up, Joes. I know you would look at me and say, 'lawdy child, you grew two sticks tall last night.' Joes, I tried readin' in your book every day, but I could not understand the words. Joes, Momma and Daddy were goin' to leave us in the fire, but Daddy saved us at the last minute. I am so sorry I let your book and note burn in the fire. I am so sorry joes." Tears came to my eyes and began to fall softly on my blouse. "I still miss you so much Joes. You left a hole in my heart. I guess you left it there so I would never forget you. I won't, I promise and yes, I remember what you said about promises. You said not to make them, because one could rarely keep them and promises are special." I stood in the middle of the room and let the love that I felt settle on me, somehow knowin' I would not be back. I crawled out of the window and made my way back to Grammy's. For the first time in my life I was free. Free from my brothers and from my Daddy. I enjoyed the wind as it swept across my face, carrying a hint of pine and honeysuckle. Summer was almost over, and I could feel a hint of fall in the breeze. This was the first time I had walked this road with so much peace. I lifted my face toward the sun and enjoyed the feel of the heat. I looked around me and noticed the pine trees that lined the road had grown, and I guess I had. Joes, he said change was good. Living with my Grammy was the best change of all. The breeze blew my hair across my eyes, and reminded me that fall was on its way. Soon it would be time to make cane syrup. I smiled as I slowly walked back to Grammy's house noticin' that my belly hadn't hurt in sometime.

Grammy taught me how to buy clothes that I could mix and match. No one had ever taken the time to show me how to dress. She had given me a new perspective on what colors would look good together. I bought my first jeans, which I could wear with different tops and two pairs of brand new shoes. My clothes fit and I felt good about the way I looked. My hair was long; down to my waist, and Grammy offered to take me to the beauty shop to have my hair cut and styled. I had never been to a beauty shop, let alone have someone else wash my hair. I was nervous stepping into the salon for the first time. I remembered the smell of perm and, how the other ladies gossiped in quiet voices. The lady was nice, and asked me how would I like it cut? I had no idea so I asked her what she thought. She decided on the feather cut. When she finished washin', cuttin', and blow dryin' my hair, she slowly turned the chair around so I could see my new hair cut for the first time. I looked in the mirror and I could not stop smilin'. My hair was shiny and beautiful, and it simply flowed. I remembered when I was younger always admiring the other girls, and wondered how their hair always looked so shiny and flowy. Now I was looking at my hair and I felt pretty. My hair looked like theirs.

Grammy said she had another surprise for me. We pulled into the parkin' lot of a store called Merle Norman, a make-up store. Wow, I didn't even know how to put on lip shine. The lady behind the counter showed me how to wear the foundation, the eye shadow, the lip shine, and the mascara. She held up the mirror for me to look at myself. I gasped and thought to myself, I look like the other girls at school and smiled at the thought. I was on cloud nine. I laid the mirror on the counter and hugged my Grammy so tight and she hugged me back. Our first hug.

"Thank you, Grammy," I whispered in her ear. Yes, this was the perfect day. As we drove home, I wondered what Joes would have thought of my new look? I casually looked at Grammy and said, "Hmmmm, I wonder what Joes would have thought of my new look?"

Grammy smiled and said, "He would think you are as beautiful now as you were when he met you when you were 4. He always said you were special, Anna Marie."

"Grammy please tell me about him. Please Grammy."

"Anna Marie, turn the radio on. Let's just be quiet for the ride home."

Grammy liked her quiet time. I did too, but darn it, I wanted answers. Grammy had known all along that Joes had known me since I was 4. Why wouldn't she tell me about him? What was the big deal? I knew he wasn't my Daddy or anything. That would cause a scandal, so why would no one talk about him? We listened to the radio and Grammy let me listen to the rock station and we rode home in our comfortable silence that we had developed between us.

Grandpa taught me how to drive his pickup truck. I was going to be 15 in a few months, and Grammy said I could get a learner's permit. I was beyond excited. New clothes, new makeup, and new hair.... just a new me, and now a learner's permit. A new life. I was over the moon.

For the first time ever, my life felt normal.

Later, school was the best it had ever been. People that I had known since first grade thought I was a new student. My new look was a success. I loved my Grammy. I felt she had given me a new life. I rode the bus home excited about my birthday. Today I would get my learner's permit. Grammy was waitin' for me as soon as I got off the bus and we drove into town so I could take the test. I passed. Grammy let me drive to the pharmacy and we sat at the counter and had a burger with a coke. Pinch me, I am dreamin', I thought.

"Anna Marie?" I knew that voice. My heart skipped a beat.

"Momma?" I said

"Anna, I would like for you to come see me. I know Frannie and the girls would love to see you as well."

I looked at Grammy, hopin' she would say I could not go, but she nodded her head.

"Sure Momma, when would be a good time?"

"How about this weekend?"

"Okay, I will see you Saturday."

"I will let Frannie know," she said.

I smiled and nodded my head. I felt sick. I wanted to forget her and Daddy both. "Grammy, why do I have to go visit Momma? You know I don't want to."

"Anna Marie, she is still your Momma and you will show her respect."

"R-e-s-p-e-c-t." I gasped. "Momma doesn't know what that is. Joes said we should treat one another the way we want to be treated. I have never treated Momma the way she has me."

"Shhhh, that is all there is to say, Anna Marie."

"Yes ma'am," I replied.

My perfect day was just ruined. My birthday, and Momma didn't even say anythin'. Why would she, she never had. Sigh. Now I had three days to dread, fret, and groan about, but I was lookin' forward to seeing Frannie and the girls.

I woke up that Saturday morning with butterflies in my belly. What would have been the perfect day was now one that I dreaded. I tried to get excited about seeing Frannie and the girls but the butterflies won. I wasn't able to eat Grammy's breakfast she had made for me. Grammy took me to Momma's house. I got out of the car and pleaded with Grammy to pick me up in two hours. "Please Grammy." She smiled and agreed.

I walked up to the front door and knocked. Frannie opened the door, and we hugged and laughed and could not talk fast enough. She asked me about school and I asked why I had not seen her this year. And then I noticed her tummy was quite round and stickin' out.

"What is wrong with you?" I asked. "Are you ill Frannie?" My heart sank, dreadin' to hear her answer. "Is this why Momma wanted me to come for a visit? You are dyin'!"I exclaimed.

"No, Anna Marie, I am not ill nor am I dyin', at least not that I know of. I am going to have a baby."

"What?" I said in complete shock. "What do you mean a baby? You are only 16, Frannie. what are you goin' to do with a baby? What about nursin' school and our dream to run away together? Who is the daddy?"

"Andy. And we did get married at the courthouse. I wanted you to be there, Annie, but Momma said no."

"No! No, Andy is our stupid neighbor down the road from Grammy's house. This does not make sense. How could Momma let this happen?" I asked as I stomped around the room while I rubbed my forehead.

"Momma is the one that encouraged me to sleep with him, Annie. She thought maybe her boyfriend would be nicer if there were a baby in the house and that I would be happier if I were with him."

"But we can still run away, Frannie, you are not stuck here. We can still have our dream."

"My dream is over Annie, at least the one we had, but you can still live your dream... maybe for both of us." She smiled a very empty, sad smile.

I hated my Momma even more at this moment.

nineteen

Molly, Diane, and I packed up the few things Momma has in her hospital room as we to take prepared her home. I let out a big sigh, thankful that I am here with her. I know that I am here by God's grace, and that He changed my heart.

When I think about the journey Momma and I have been on, I know first-hand just how powerful forgiveness is and the true meaning of a Heavenly Father's love. This revelation did not come easy for me. I wanted to argue with God and tell him how justified I was to feel the way I did. How I was abandoned, beaten, raped, and neglected. When I first gave my heart to God, I would say "but God," when He would lay something on my heart and I could hear Him whisper back to me, "I know. I was there. I saw it all that is why I am placing you here with your Momma. She needs you, Anna Marie, because you know and understand the abandonment. You understand the need for unconditional love." I smiled, thankful that God won that argument. But I wasn't always a willing pupil.

twenty

Sayin' goodbye to Frannie was hard. I left feelin' confused and angry. Confused by life and the purpose of our existence. And angry at my Momma, how could she do this to Frannie? She told my oldest sister she should get pregnant because that would be the only way she could ever get out of the house. It seems my Momma wants everyone around her to be as miserable as she is. I told Grammy this theory and she said I should not be so hard on my Momma. Why would Grammy defend a person who does not like her? And Joes, I know he would be tellin' me the same thing. "Little Anna," he would say, "never judge someone, you don't knows where they have been." What does that even mean? Now that I am older, I would ask Joes, if he were here. He had a way of explainin' things to me that I would understand. He was so smart.

Regardless of what she thought of Momma, I was thankful I was at my Grammy's house. I loved it there because for once I felt life was good, peaceful, and right. For a change, school was great and my grades were gettin' better as my confidence grew. I felt like I could conquer the world. But then, before the end of the school year, my Daddy showed up one day out of the blue. No phone call, no warnin', he was just there when I got home from school. When I saw him my heart dropped and so did my confidence. When I saw him my shoulders drooped and my heart began to beat fast. I felt my confidence disappear. I knew he was here for me but I could not figure out why; the man hated me. Why would he not leave me alone?

"Anna, we have come back for you," he said.

"Why?" I asked, "Why can't you leave me alone. I love it here with Grammy." I replied as tears welled up behind my eyelids.

"Anna," Grammy answered, "you can come back and visit anytime." Grammy always makin' things seem like they are not so bad when in reality they were horrible.

"Get your things and leave your make-up, no need for such nonsense." I glared at him, as I passed him to gather my things. This time, things were going to be different. I would not let him or his girlfriend beat me again.

As we pulled out of the driveway, Daddy's girlfriend explained the reason I was being taken back to the hell I thought I had escaped. Sittin' in the back seat of the car, Daddy's girlfriend turned back to look at me with a smile as she told me she needed my help in the restaurant she and Daddy were openin'.

And she said, "You will do this for no pay because you are family. Right dear?" As she patted my Daddy's leg. He nodded in agreement.

They also gathered up my three younger sisters on the way back to their place. I was so mad I was shakin'. I studied my Daddy from the back seat. I don't understand him or Momma. He did not seem any happier with his new girlfriend than he did with Momma. And Momma always had bruises on her from her boyfriend. Momma and Daddy did argue a lot but Daddy never hit her. Yet, this man beats her, until one time he put her in the hospital. I wondered why she chose to stay.

The four of us girls got settled into Daddy's house. I hid my make-up and put it on after I got to school and took it off before I got home. Right after school, me and my sisters went directly to the restaurant and worked until ten o'clock every night. I still managed to find time to do my homework but my grades were not as good as they had been. I was back to hatin' my life and after awhile I quit wearin' make-up and stylin' my hair. What was the point?

School was out and our summer was goin' to be spent at the restaurant, from the time they opened until they closed. My youngest sister was the luckiest of the four of us. My Daddy's girlfriend seemed to like her, so she would take her home and bathe her and put her to bed, while we cleaned and prepared the restaurant for the next day's business. I decided I didn't mind being at the restaurant, it was better than being at home and being abused. As before when I worked in the restaurant, I loved the people, and I had a knack for runnin' and makin' decisions in this line of work. Some people would say I have a business sense about me. I liked hearin' that. It gave me hope that I would be able to take care of myself.

Comin' home late with my Daddy's girlfriend one night she began to complain about my work. I knew she just wanted to pick on me, so I ignored her. After a while when she did not get a rise out of me she reached over and slapped me in the face. I was startled and without hesitation, I punched her in the arm. She began to yell at me. I tuned her out feelin' the hand print she left on my cheek begin to sting. We parked and I jumped out of the car and she followed me as she continued to yell at me. I walked in the house straight back to the bedroom and packed the few things I had in a brown paper bag.

She yells, "What do you think you are doin'?"

"I am leavin' here. I will never come back. You are a witch."

I stormed out of the house not knowin' where I was goin', but knowin' I would not stand for another beatin' from my dad when he got home. No, that was over, no one will ever be physical with me again. I watched my Momma over the last few years livin' with her boyfriend as he abused her and put her in the hospital more times than I cared to remember. I heard my Daddy's girlfriend screamin' at me to come back and that if I did she would not say a word to my Daddy about our argument, just come back. I smiled, as I heard the fear in her voice. What would she tell Daddy? At the end of the day, would he even care or would he be relieved?

It was dark, no moon, and the stars decided to hide behind a thick layer of clouds.

"Joes?" I whispered. "Where do I go?" I missed him as a deep loneliness and sadness settled in my heart once again. I knew he would have good advice for me, but all I got was silence and the only answers I got back were the crickets and night frogs croakin' out what sounds like the song, "RESPECT". I smiled as I thought of all the days spent on Joes' front porch sippin' his sweet tea and listenin' to his stories about Jesus always rememberin' to speak like a proper lady. I had not thought about Joes Jesus for a long time. I did talk to Him and asked Him to take me away from this family that never loved me, but He never did and the beatin's continued and actually got worse with my Daddy's girlfriend. So I quit talkin' to Him and wondered if Joes could see me and if his Jesus was real, why He did not like me?

I did not ponder this for long as I had to make a decision about where to go and how I would take care of myself. I couldn't go back to Grammy's house. Daddy would look for me there. I let out a big sigh. Not sure about what the future holds but knowin' anythin' had to be better than what was behind me. I looked down the long dark road excited about my future and for a brief moment, I wondered if I could do this. The answer came back as a resounding "yes." How? I did not know, but I walked fearless into the night holdin' my brown bag, smilin' as the feelin' of freedom and the expectations of my future were as long as the road ahead...waitin' to be written.

twenty-one

I get the call late on a Tuesday night.

"It is Frannie, Annie," she says, "I know you have only been home a couple of days, but Momma has taken a turn for the worse. She is asking for you."

"Okay," I whisper, as I open my eyes and squint to see the time while trying to get my senses about me. "What do I need to do? Should I leave now? If I drive, I have 16 hours ahead of me. I guess I could fly, but you know how I hate that."

"You probably have time to drive. I will see you in a couple of days. And Annie, Momma said she does not trust anyone but you to give her medicine. She won't take it until you get here."

I sigh, "Okay, I will leave tonight."

I refresh my suitcases; I have not fully unpacked them for two and a half years. Always on standby, ready to run back if Momma needed me. To say my children and my husband have been champs throughout this process would be an understatement. They understood the journey God has taken me on. My kids only know bits and pieces of my childhood and the relationship with my parents has all but been non-existence. They never really have asked questions. It was just the way it was. Andrew, my husband was out of town on business. I call the nanny to come over. I would be leaving in a few hours and she was always so gracious to me. She never complained, she was just always there, a true Godsend. I give her a brief schedule for the boys and remind her to always set the alarm at night before bed. She smiled and I laugh knowing I give her the same speech every time.

As I drive the car down my tree lined driveway and wait for the gate to open I look out over the 20 acre estate that my husband and I just bought. Seven years before we bought it, we were out for a stroll. I told him that day, when this house comes on the market we are buying it. He laughed. Now seven years later, we own this beautiful estate.

The roads my life has taken...

Walking down the dirt roads of Alabama in the middle of the night to escape the abuse of my childhood, the uncertainty of the future that night, all of it has led me to this moment.

The forgiveness God showered on me, His love for me, empowered me to find forgiveness for my Momma. I am blessed. The gate opens and I pull my Mercedes onto the road and head to the only place open at 2 a.m. for a cup of coffee. I put my favorite CD in and turn it on low. My mind is already beginning to drift as it does on these long drives. Andrew, my husband and best friend, came into my life 15 years ago. We met as both of us were going through a divorce. My husband had left and his wife had left. We met at church on a Wednesday night during prayer service. If he tells the story on how we met he will tell you I stalked him. We laugh every time he tells the story. Our life has been full of laughter and learning about how to have a Godly marriage. We have had our share of struggles and growing pains, but we're committed to one another and giving up is not an option. No matter how hard it got. Andrew came into my life as I had given up on marriage. I was content to raise my two sons, Henry and Christopher and my daughter Victoria Ann on my own. When Andrew and I met, I was struggling to write my first Christian novel and building up my home decorating business. Andrew is a successful businessman and real estate developer. We had a whirlwind romance and on the night he proposed to me he took my hand and said, "Anna Marie, if you will marry me, I will spend the rest of my life protecting you, encouraging you, and loving you." Andrew knew little of my past but enough to know I had trust issues. I would share more as our marriage became stronger. He hates that I had been robbed of my childhood. He makes a point to make a big deal out of birthdays and Christmas. He is a great stand in dad to my kids, he adores them and they adore him in return. I love that we have given our marriage to God, and He is still writing our story, one chapter at a time. My Momma never met Andrew. Of course she has only been back in my life for the last two years. He had offered many times to come along with me, but I always told him I needed this time alone with my Momma. He understood.

I know that this will be my last trip back to see Momma. I know she does not have long and I probably should not have left her. But it had been 3 weeks since I had been home. I was missing my kids and husband. As always the guilt thing pulled at me, when I am home I need to be with her and when I am with her I need to be home with them. To say my emotions have been all over the place since I got the phone call two years ago about her being sick, would be an understatement. As I pull out to begin the journey, my mind goes back to the night I decided to leave it all behind......

twenty-two

I thought about goin' back and livin' in Joes' place, but remembered the last time I saw it, the front porch was all but collapsin' in on itself. No, I could not go back, I had to move forward. I lived on the streets behind a restaurant in cardboard boxes after I ran away from my Daddy's house. It was no surprise that no one came to look for me. I don't recall how long I lived in my cardboard box home. I would go through the scraps they tossed out at night. You would be surprised at the half eaten fried chicken or half eaten BBQ sandwiches I would find. It was a feast. A hose was hooked up, so I had runnin' water and was able to drink and bathe somewhat. It was better than my brother's peed bathwater.

One day I was brave enough to go inside and ask the owner for a job.

He said, "Are you the kid livin' in the back of my place?"

"Yes I am," I answered back with my chin pointed high.

He laughed and said I had a job. "It's hard work. Do you think you are up for it?"

I replied with a very determined, "yes."

So I begin the 5 a.m. work duties before I headed off to school. After school, I would walk back to the restaurant and work until closin' at 10. The couple who owned the restaurant also owned the apartments next to the restaurant, so I was allowed to move into one as part of my pay. It was one room with a bathroom. I felt like I was livin' in a mansion. It was mine. A safe place to come home to after school and work. I had no one to tell me what to do or how to do it. After I had worked for a few months and saved up some money, I bought new sheets and a spread for my bed. I felt like a princess. I had saved enough money to buy a second hand chair and television set.

Joes would have been proud of me. I worked hard that summer, takin' what I had learned from Tizzy about meal plannin' and bein' creative, payin' attention to schedulin', and learnin' how to cook. The owners took notice and promoted me to night manager. It came natural to me. I kept the wait staff in line. Nothin' walked out the back door and the cash register always balanced. Another year came and went and I turned 16. The owners of the restaurant gave me a used car as a gift for all my hard work. I could not believe it. I felt like a normal 16 year old.

I was thankful for their gift, but it came with a price. The owner showed up at my place late one Saturday night with the smell of alcohol on his breath and wanted to have sex. He said, "You didn't think the car was for all your hard work did you?" I was able to fend him off with the threat of tellin' his wife. So after many attempts of him tryin', I told him that not only would I tell his wife I would tell the police, and he back handed me across the face. So I packed up my things and left in the middle of the night. Once again not sure what the future would hold or where I would go, but one thing became very clear, nothin' is ever what it seems and you can trust no one.

twenty-three

I had been driving for four hours and needed a break. I pull into the gas station to take care of all my needs and instead of driving, I pull over to the side of the store to let my back rest and hopefully take a 15 minute nap. My mind is on full speed, memories racing by so fast until it decides to land on one, I have no choice but to accommodate.

I had successfully, over the years, been able to completely block memories from my past. I found them of no use and they would only bring anger, bitterness, and unforgiveness into my present, so I kept them tightly locked up. When Momma became ill, the memories refused to stay locked up. But what I have learned is that God is the one that brings new insight to them, giving them a place in my life, learning about forgiveness and love, and that they can indeed be a learning tool. So the memory of Momma telling me how much she did not like me is the one that wins tonight. Oh Momma, I sigh, as I let the memory of her words saturate my body, my heart, my emotions, and my spirit.

Over the years my life has taken many turns and twists. The one thing that follows you from childhood to adulthood is the yearning for your parents' love, affection, affirmation, approval and yes, even a relationship them. All the things I did not and still do not have, but yet keep seeking. I would reach out time and time again over many years of trying to develop some sort of connection with my Momma and Daddy, all of them ending with heartache.

"Anna Marie," I can hear my Momma like it was today, "why do you bother with coming over here. I have told you time and time again, I don't like you, and you make me nervous. You always were a peculiar child and nothing has changed now that you are an adult."

"Yes Momma, I know you tell me that quite often. But I am your child, don't you want to know who I am? I want to know you. Aren't you curious about what has happened in my life? Don't you want to know your granddaughter and your grandsons? Do you even remember their names?" Momma just sits at her kitchen table, her fingers tapping the table. I look around her tiny house, cigarette smoke clinging to the ceiling, country music playing in the background, nothing much has changed in her life. She had finally left her abusive boyfriend. She was all alone, except, for Frannie. She and the other kids would come by and spend time with her.

I sighed. Why do I even try? I picked up my coat and I headed for the door, as my hand reached for the doorknob, she very quietly said to me, "I do need some money if you have any extra on you." My hand stopped short of opening the door and I turned to look at her. She spoke quickly to defend herself, "It is not like you don't have any to spare. Look at that car you are driving and the fancy clothes you have on. You are supposed to take care of your parents." I almost laughed out loud at her words, but instead I reached into my purse and took out a couple of hundred dollar bills and laid them in front of her. I snapped my wallet shut and she jumped, startled. I started to say something, but instead walked back to the door and this time she did not stop me, because she got what she wanted. I reached for the door slowly, hoping that this would be the time she would say, "I love you. Please don't go. Let's work on this." But all I got was silence.

I pulled out of the driveway as tears spilled down onto my silk blouse, regretting the attempt, and like always made myself a promise, I would not try again. But knowing I would.

Why do I keep trying? It was obvious the woman hated me. I know without a doubt she was my Momma. My father, I was not sure of, but of her I am. I left with a deep sadness.

I thought of my own daughter and the joy she has brought into my life. I cannot imagine not cuddling her when she was a baby, rocking her to sleep, singing lullabies to her, loving her, protecting her, wanting to be in her life. I die inside thinking about life without her. Not a day goes by that we don't have a quick call just to say hi if nothing else. I remember her at age four looking at how helpless she was, remembering Joes and the watermelon patch. How I wandered off from the house for hours at a time and no one caring. Watching her turn eight, and remembering "the thing" that happen to me at that age and me telling Momma, the one person that was supposed to protect me, but how she left me to defend myself. I knew I would kill anyone who ever touched my daughter like that. Remembering all the beatings Daddy gave me and Momma watching him with a smile on her face. How I wanted to run away and find a family that loved me. Why Joes Jesus would not protect me and take me away like the wind carrying the snowflake to the perfect place before it would release it. How I wanted to end my life because it made no sense, it had no purpose. The people you trusted turned out to use, or abuse you. I found no one I could trust and my life had no purpose, until I met Jesus.

Yes, I finally met Joes' Jesus.

twenty-four

    My life has been one with a lot of mistakes and regrets. When I met Joes' Jesus, I was going through one of my many divorces. My life, up until this point included several failed attempts at marriage. But out of those failed attempts, I had my daughter and two wonderful sons. They were my heartbeat. I knew the moment I saw my daughter's sonogram that I would lay down my life for her. A fierce emotion of protection erupted throughout my physical and emotional being, unlike anything I had ever experienced. My life changed forever with her birth as it did with my two sons; that same fierceness to protect, to love, to hold them close. I did not know how to be married, the one thing in life I never conquered, until I met Andrew. But motherhood came as easy for me as putting on make-up. It was the one thing I did not fail at.

    I remember like it was yesterday, the day I met Joes' Jesus. I had just received divorce papers from my estranged husband. I looked down at the papers and began to cry. "Why?" I asked an empty room, "Why can I not get it right? There has got to be more to life than broken relationships, mistrust, and people taking advantage of you and using you. What do You want from me?" I asked an empty room, not talking to anyone as my words echoed throughout the room, the only response I got was the ticking of the clock. "What?" I screamed as my legs gave out from underneath me. I slid down to the wood floor in the entry of this grand house, cleaned by my housekeeper. All the material grandeur money could buy, and I am left to sink into my own misery, tears that will not stop, emotions that go from self-pity to anger. I am not sure how long I was on the floor. By this time I was in a fetal position weeping and dry heaving, like I had lost my best friend. Lost in uncertainties, not sure what life is supposed to be about. Why does this divorce bother me so much? I have always prided myself on the theory, I will not beg you to stay. If you don't want to be here, then go, the door is wide open. It is not like I loved my husband, that died a long time ago. Five years without marital touching, living in the same house as roommates. No, this emotion was not about him leaving. It was more. It was an emotion that was coming from the depths of my soul. An emptiness that was unbearable and a loneliness that threatened to overtake me. A hole in my heart that was bigger than when Joes died, and bigger than when Grammy went to be with Joes. This emotion was raw, untouched, searching, seeking; but for what?

I cried out again, "What do You want?" I am not sure who I was talking to, but this time, I heard Joes' voice, the one voice I trusted. The only voice I have ever trusted. The voice that I have missed. I hung my head in shame, from whom, I am not sure. I had not thought of Joes for years. The thought of hearing his voice penetrates a sadness and loneliness that I was not aware I had been carrying all these years.

"Joes." I answered. "Oh Joes, I have made a mess of my life. What is the point of going on? What is my purpose? I wish you were here Joes, I really do. I am sorry I have not thought of you in years. Too ashamed, I guess. Knowing you would be disappointed." I sat on the floor waiting to hear his voice again, silence. I fell asleep only to be awakened by Joes voice. I sat up, looking for him, disoriented, feeling confused. Did I imagine it? No there it was again, only this time the voice is not Joes.

"I am here, Little Anna, I have always been here."

Joes' Jesus!

So now you want to make an appearance? Now? I let my anger over take me, as I yell at Joes Jesus. "I begged You to take me away from the parents who hated me, from the "thing", from all the abuse, but you did nothing. You left me all alone. You let all the things I asked you to take me away from, happen! You left me in all of them. Answer me!" I yelled.

"Every time I would see the wind carry the snowflake, it would not let it drop until it found the right place, the perfect place, I begged you to take me away like the snowflake. But you left me there every time, every time!"

"I was there, Little Anna, always. I waited for you to ask Me into your heart. You never did."

"So why now?" I asked.

"Because you were talking to me"

"No I was talking to Joes. Not you."

"Every time you talked to Joes, Little Anna, you were talking to me. I sent Joes to you."

"No, no I do not understand." I covered my hands over my ears. Nothing's making sense.

"Little Anna, I was with you in the fire I was with you the night the owner came to you for favors. I was with you and your sister Frannie the night you asked Me to let your mother live. I was with you the night your Momma's boyfriend was holding your Momma down with a gun pointed to her head; you were the little girl on her knees. I heard you. I let your mother live and I gave you the daughter you wanted. You had close calls but nothing ever happened to you again. Do you remember? I am waiting for you, Little Anna Marie, when you were on your knees, you asked me not to forget you, I never have."

I weep as the memories engulf me. All along it was You. All along it was You I was seeking to fill the hole in my heart. The hole I have been lost in since Joes died. It is You I want, it is You I need. Then silence, and Joes Jesus quit talking to me. The emptiness took the place of the warmth I was feeling. No, I don't want the emptiness anymore. "Please," I whispered, "I need You, Joes Jesus. Come into my life. Forgive me of my sins. You are all I need."

"I am here Little Anna."

I wept for what seemed like an eternity until I could not weep anymore. I stood on wobbly legs, knowing but not knowing my life had been changed forever. I was not sure what would lie ahead. I never was. But as I looked at the woman in the mirror, her eyes black with make-up, I knew with certainty that I would never be alone again and the hole in my heart began to fill up with a love that I would never be able to explain. Joes' Jesus was now my Jesus.

twenty-five

I can't take a cat nap. The memories are rushing like a dam about to burst. I gave up and pulled out of the parking lot and begin the drive to Mommas again as another memory pushes it way through all the others.......

My phone rang and it was Momma.

I had not talked to her for six months.

"Anna," her voice was weak.

"Yes Momma?" I say, hoping she cannot hear the surprise in my voice.

"Why have you not been back to see me?" She asked.

"Well, Momma..." I wanted to scream at her! I wanted to say all the things I was feeling, the hurt, the sadness, and have her answer all the "whys" but instead I said, "I do have a company to run, the boys and Andrew at home. I am sending the money to cover all the expenses that come up, did I miss something?"

"No Anna, you did not miss anythin', but I want you to take care of me. I want you to be here."

There is a long silence that seems to go on forever as I process what she said. Is she demanding it or needing it? I am not sure, but I could hear God saying to me, "She is asking for you. Go to her."

"Sure Momma, I will be there in a couple of days."

All she said was "okay," and hung up the phone.

I sat there for what seemed like a lifetime. I do not understand. I am not sure why she wants me to be the one to take care of her. All of the emotions come flooding back. I pray a quick prayer, for God to give me the strength to be the daughter I know I am supposed to be. I pack my suitcases and head back to Illinois.

twenty-six

Oh Momma, hang on. I am on my way. The guilt of leaving her came crashing down on me. I pray for God's peace to surround me as I know I need to be strong for Frannie. I begin to focus on the things I know I will have to take care of. Frannie had already asked if I would take care of the funeral arrangements. She said, "You are stronger than me. Annie, you always have been." Tender hearted and soft spoken Frannie, she was close to Momma. Frannie and Momma found a place of contentment with one another years ago. We never talked about it because Frannie knew how hard I had tried and how Momma had refused my offers, except for the money that she was always willing to take. I cannot blame her. I was always giving it to her, somehow, hoping that would bring her to me. It never did. It is true that old saying: money can buy you many things, but love is not one of them. I thought many times, she could have at least pretended she liked me. I would have settled for that, but Momma would not even appease me with pretending.

I pull into Momma's driveway and Frannie comes out to meet me. Her face is swollen and eyes are puffy from crying. I hug her neck and ask how Momma is doing. "Oh Annie, it won't be long. Momma has been asking for you."

I walk into Momma's small apartment. All of my siblings are in the living room. I stagger backwards at the emotions running through my heart. When was the last time we were all in the same room? We are here, except for my brother Mike--- the one that was meaner than a snake as a young boy.

Mike was killed in combat in Afghanistan. He enlisted when he was eighteen. He wrote Frannie years later just to touch base. Mike had married a girl named Alice and they had one daughter. In the letter he asked Frannie to ask me to forgive him. Frannie had asked what he meant by that, but I never told her. But I asked when she wrote him back to tell him I forgave him a long time ago. I miss Mike. He became a wonderful husband and father and a believer in Joes' Jesus. After Frannie wrote and told him I had forgiven him, he called. We talked for hours in between the tears and laughter. The boy became a man....one who didn't make excuses for his behavior as a boy, but owned his mistakes. He was as much a victim of our childhood as I was.

Jack, my older brother is married and has three daughters. Jack came to know and walk with Jesus before Mike did. In fact, Jack led Mike to The Lord. My sisters are also doing well. Nell, my oldest sister, finished school and became an elementary teacher. Diane has a successful beauty salon business with several locations. Molly is single and a flight attendant. She loves to travel and intends to see the world before she settles down. Shelly is my shopping buddy. She and her husband have a chain of Chinese restaurants. And then there is my sweet pinky promise Frannie, who married so young, but God has a way of working things out. She and Andy are still happily married with two children. Most of all my sisters have come to know the Lord, and I am still in complete trust that that the ones who have not yet made the decision to follow Christ will do so.

As I look around the room, I know Jesus has been good to us. The way we started in life, the brokenness, the poverty, the abuse and to be standing here today with my siblings and to see where we are at in life is a miracle. Frannie takes me back to Momma's bedroom. I look at her lying there with her purple blanket and I sit on the edge of the bed. I reach over and take her hand. I caress her cheek and lean in to whisper to her three simple words that took me a long time to actually mean: "I love you." She smiles and squeezes my hand. I want to believe with all my heart that was her way of saying "I love you," back.

"Will you stay in here with me for a little while?" she asks

"Of course, Momma, let me get a few things from the car and I will be right back." She closes her eyes and Frannie and I walk out to the car to grab my overnight bag. Frannie begins to cry and I hold her for a few minutes. "Frannie, it is going to be okay."

She nods and we walk back into the house. She stays with the siblings and I walk back to Momma's bedroom. I pull a chair next to Momma's bed and she seems to be sleeping. I take my Bible out and begin to read. I am not sure how long I was reading before I looked up and saw Momma looking at me. I laid the Bible down and took her hand.

"Are you reading your Bible, Anna Marie?" she asked.

"Yes, Momma. Momma are you saved?"

"Anna, I told you before I was saved when I was a little girl."

"Would you like to rededicate your life to The Lord, Momma? Momma? Momma?" Her eyes were closed and she wasn't breathing. How could it happen so fast? So quickly? I grab Momma's hand and raise my voice again, "Momma?" Frannie runs back into the room followed by the rest of the siblings.

"Frannie will you call the doctor, please?" I asked.

Jack came around to the other side of the bed and took Momma's pulse.

"Anna Marie, I think she is gone," Jack whispered.

"She was just talking, she can't be gone." It is really hard for me to process that she really is gone. "Jack, are you sure? I have so many questions I still want to ask her. I need to know who my biological father is. I wanted to ask her why, why didn't she love me? Jack, I need to know." Jack came around and put his arms around me and told me it didn't matter who my Dad was. We have each other; the seven of us. We have each other and you have Andrew, Victoria Ann, Christopher and Henry.

"She loved you, Anna Marie, she just didn't know how to show you. She told me she wanted to tell you many times, but she was afraid too much time had gone by. Anna Marie, you are the one she wanted here. It was always you. She loved you." Jack let me cry on his shoulder until I could cry no more. The deep sadness I felt was for the things that could have been, the time that was wasted, and hugs that were never given.

The ambulance came and pick up Momma and took her to the funeral home. Everything became a whirlwind after that. Andrew and the children flew up to Illinois. The funeral was on a cool Saturday afternoon. The sun was bright and the leaves had a touch of red and orange to them, reminding us fall was just around the corner. As the preacher was speaking, I took a deep breath and exhaled slowly. I am not sure of the exact moment when all the anger left or I stopped asking "why me?" I do remember when I looked at my Momma and felt genuine love for her. God will do that when He gets into your heart. When you accept His love and realize how much He has forgiven you, it becomes easier to forgive.

The road I traveled to have her accept me, love me, and acknowledge me was a hard and sometimes a hopeless one. The journey was to never have the perfect, happy ending I was seeking. So, in the end, I settled for the fact that she wanted me with her when she passed. Tears began to build up behind my sunglasses and slide down my cheek. Andrew squeezed my hand and wrapped his pinky around my pinky. This was our secret "I love you" without saying anything.

The crowd of people consisting of extended family and friends had left the gravesite and the seven of us were saying goodbye when I looked up and saw the man I have called Dad all my life standing under an oak tree a few feet away from Momma's grave. I nudge Jack and we walk over to where he was standing.

"Dad, what are you doing here?" I asked, realizing I haven't seen him in years. Not since he told me I wasn't his daughter.

"I wanted to see how you kids were doing," he said.

Jack says, "Well, Dad, we are glad you came. Why don't you come over to my house, everyone will be there."

"Okay, I can do that. Are you okay with that Anna Marie?"

"Sure Dad," I whispered, as my knees were shaking with so much emotion. Jack puts his arm around me and tells me it will be okay.

I walk back to where Andrew and the kids are and he puts his arms around me. "Was that your Dad?" He asked in a low voice so the kids wouldn't hear. I nod my head yes. "You don't have to go if you aren't ready," Andrew said.

"No, I need to go."

We walk into Jack's house, as I made my way through the crowd of family members' hugs and well wishes. I step into the kitchen and the man I had called Dad all my life was standing next to the backdoor. I shake my head trying to come to grips with the situation.

Dad looks up at me and says, "Anna, can we step outside to talk?"

I shake my head yes and step out onto the back porch.

"I am not sure where to begin," he said.

"Let me start," I say. "First of all, thank you for coming today. I know it means a lot to the other kids and to me." I added slowly. Dad shakes his head but doesn't look at me, "Dad, I am sorry. I don't know what else to call you." An awkward silence takes the place of us struggling to find a firm place to begin a conversation. I wrap my arms around myself as the late afternoon breeze blows softly against my bare arms. The younger children are playing in the back yard and in the distance, a car alarm is going off.

Finally, he looks up at me and says, "You can call me Dad if you want to, Anna. I know it has been hard for you since I told you that you weren't my daughter. I was hard on you Anna. I reckon if I were being honest, I was mean to you. I took a lot of my anger out on you. One day I hope you can find it in your heart to forgive me. I don't expect it right now, but maybe one day." He looks at me with tears building up in his eyes. "I don't deserve your forgiveness, but one day, maybe one day, I can earn it. Your forgiveness. A man grows wiser in his old age Anna, he can see things clearly when he gives his heart to The Lord. God has given me a second chance with your siblings. I hope we can have a second chance."

I look at the man who was so mean to me. The man I couldn't wait to get away from. The man who is not my father, but who wants a second chance. Tears slip down my cheeks as my childhood flashes before me, the beatings, the insults, and the fear. I look into my Dad's eyes and know he is a changed man. God will do that to a person.

And just like with my Momma, God gave me a genuine love for this man I call Dad. Forgiveness flooded my heart as the tears continue to fall like a soft spring rain.

"I can forgive you," I whispered. "It will take a while for the trust to come but I am willing to take it one day at a time, if that is okay?" The tears that had been welling up in his eyes but never fell, begin to run like a dam. A new beginning to an old story, a story waiting to be rewritten. It's like an eraser that erases the mistakes on paper. When we are willing, God will erase the mistakes in our lives and give us a second chance. But it takes willing hearts.

"I will take that, Anna. Thank you for giving an old man a chance to prove he is more than what he was."

"Dad," I paused for what seemed like an eternity, "do you know who my biological father is? It won't change our relationship and what we are building on. I just need to know."

He looked at me with so much sadness in his eyes as he lets out a long sigh. "I don't know Anna. I wish I could give you that. Your Momma never told me. I am sorry."

Jack and Andrew came out to check on us. Andrew puts his arms around me and whispered, "You okay?" I nodded as I relaxed and found comfort in his embrace.

As we gather our things to leave Jack's house, we made plans to spend Thanksgiving together. All of us, including Dad.

twenty-seven

Andrew walks into the kitchen with the mail. It has been three months since Mom's funeral. Things finally seem to be getting back to normal. I am sitting at the breakfast bar enjoying my morning coffee, reading through emails from my book publisher who says we should be hearing from the movie producer soon. I am still in awe that someone is looking at my manuscript for a movie before the book comes out next summer. The phone rings and I see it is my dad. I smile as I reach for the phone to answer his call.

My Dad and I talk on the phone once a week. The trust is slowly beginning to build and we have slipped into an ease with each other. We talk briefly about Christopher, Henry and Victoria Ann. He always wants updates, and of course, his love to Andrew. And a reminder not to forget to come in a day early so we can stay one night with him over the Thanksgiving holidays.

"Anna Marie?" Andrew says as I hang up the phone.

I look up at Andrew. "Yes?" I smiled as he stands at the end of the breakfast bar sorting the mail, thinking how blessed I am that he is in my life.

"Do you know an attorney by the name of David Tallon?"

"No, I don't' think so. Maybe it is about the movie deal. Open it!" I say with excitement.

Andrew opens it and begins to read and stops in mid sentence, "Anna, this isn't about your book. You need to read this." I reach for the letter and begin to read in disbelief. Mr. David Tallon is requesting a meeting next week with me in regards to an inheritance from my biological father. Would I please call his secretary to set a day and time.

"Andrew, what do I do?" I hand him the letter back with shaky hands.

"Call. Make the appointment. Anna, this is something you have waited your whole life for. You will finally know who your father is."

"Andrew, he is dead. I won't know him. He's gone." I begin to cry. I had so many questions. If he knew about me, then why not contact me? Why leave me an inheritance and never call me or reach out to me? So many mixed emotions are swirling through my mind.

I waited a few days before calling to set the appointment. Andrew and I flew to South Carolina to meet with Mr. Tallon.

We walk into his office on the 20th floor of a posh building. Everything was impeccable and well decorated. Mr. Tallon was well dressed, sitting behind a very large desk and looked to be in his seventies. He stands and greets us and has us take a seat.

"Mr. and Mrs. Davenport, thank you for meeting me. I am sure this comes as a surprise and shock to you, Mrs. Davenport."

"I do have a lot of questions, Mr. Tallon."

"I am sure you do. Let me first start by saying you are the sole heir to Mr. Blakely's entire estate. He had no other children or survivors. His wife passed a year ago and he had no desire to leave his estate to anyone other than you, his daughter. The estate consists of his business and real estate holdings. The business is Blakely's Shipping, the largest import/export shipping in the United States. I am sure you have heard of it. Real Estate holdings include Hampton, Hawaii, and Florida and his 200 acre estate here in South Carolina. He also had a 20 car collection of various antique Mercedes and Corvettes which is at the 200 acre estate known as The Bella. This also includes his yacht the "Anna Marie" and business real estate property including the building you are sitting in and his vast collection of cigar pipes from around the world. He has also set up trust accounts for your children and any future great grandchildren I know this is a lot to take in, so I will leave you for a few minutes and will return to answer any questions you may have.

I sat there in shock, first to learn who my father is, and then to learn about the inheritance.

Of course I have heard of Ralph Blakey. Who hasn't? He is a self-made billionaire.

But, how and when did he and my Momma meet?

Mr. Tallon walks back in before Andrew and I had a chance to even catch our breath, let alone talk to one another.

"Mr. Tallon, I want to know..... when did my father know about me? How long has he known?"

"Mrs. Davenport, I believe the answers you are seeking are in this letter your father left to you. But the short answer is when you were three. If memory serves me, I believe your mother came to him to ask if he would raise you. There was a meeting in my office, that was when I first met Mr. Blakely. Mrs. Blakely, your Father's wife, wanted children, but could not have them and the thought of raising her husband's child from an affair was too much for her. Your mother and father saw each other many times, and for a long time. However, he wouldn't leave his wife. Mrs. Blakely wouldn't have anything to do with the situation. She forbade him to see you or have any contact with you. When she passed a year ago, he wanted to reach out to you, but figured too much time had passed and he was a sick man as well. He had a weak heart and died of a heart attack a couple of weeks ago. He was very clear about his wishes for you. Arrangements have been made for you and Mr. Davenport if you would like to stay at The Bella. The house staff is waiting for you and a driver is downstairs. We can meet again tomorrow. I will come to the estate around ten in the morning."

I nodded to the arrangement and Andrew and I left.

The phone rang and it was my Dad. I answered and he asked how I was. I had called him to let him know about the letter and that Andrew and I had flown to South Carolina to meet with the attorney.

"Anna, you are going to be okay? Don't let the "whys" fill your heart with anger. Have you read the letter yet?"

"No," I answered.

"Read the letter, Anna. Find the answers you have longed for. Forgive him Anna for not being there for you. Hear his heart. Okay?"

"I will try, Dad." I choked back tears.

We pulled onto a tree lined road that led to what I can only describe as a "Gone With The Wind" kind of house. It was breathtaking. The house staff came out to greet us and, Mary, the house manager, showed us the entire estate. She showed us to our room and informed us dinner would be at six sharp.

Andrew and I finally had a moment to ourselves and we can't even speak. We were overwhelmed by what God had already blessed us with in our lives: we have a great marriage, children, his real estate development company, acreage, family, and so much more. Why would we need even more than what we have? As I ask, I can hear Joes telling me that one day his Jesus would restore to me even more than I could hope, dream, or imagine.

I take a photo of my Father from the library downstairs and stared into his eyes. I have his eyes and nose. I can see me in him. I wonder what kind of man he was. Was he soft spoken or abrupt? Was he liked by his house staff? His employees? This person, this man, I have dreamed of my whole life and now I am standing in his house that he has left to me, but I don't know him. His eyes stare back at me but I have no sense of who he was. Just a picture of a man that I have no history with. How can I connect to him?

I sit the picture down and take out the letter he had written me.

I open it and begin to read. It was a long letter; it revealed his heart about me and my mother. He built this business for me. He collected all these things for me. Hoping one day he would be able to share them with me. He loved my mother but could not bring himself to leave his wife. He and my Mom parted ways after a six year affair. She would bring me with her when they would meet. But I have no memory of him. Why can't I remember him? He asked for my forgiveness and expressed the sorrow of not knowing me. Hoping that my inheritance would somehow make up for him not being in my life. The letter went on, but one part really stood out:

Anna, I know you remember Joe. He was my friend. This may come as a shock to you Anna, but I made a deal with your Grammy years ago to allow Joe to live there for as long as he was alive. I bought that farm for you Anna. It is yours. It is included with all the property that you have inherited. Joe and I met when I was seeing your mother. He kept our secret and he never told anyone. He kept a watch over you, Anna. He called you his Little Anna. He would give me updates on you. He was a good man. He loved you. I am sorry Anna for all your pain. Pain I could not protect you from. Forgive an old man for being a fool.

The last page of the letter was a copy of a photo of him and me when I was 2.5. He is looking at me and smiling, love in his eyes.

Remember me this way Anna as I look at you in this picture, I pray you see my love for you.

twenty-eight

"Little Anna," Joes says as he is lifting me up in the air. "You grew two sticks tall today." I laugh as he lifts me higher in the air.

I awaken from my dream of Joes. Dreams I have more often, always filled with the sense of love and protection. I know he was my best friend, my protector, and my teacher. He was the first person who loved me, and whom I loved.

Before Grammy passed away she did tell me about Joes. Joes' Daddy, worked for my great Grandpa. Joes has always lived on the backside of Grammy's farm. Joes married and had a daughter, but Joes' wife and daugher were killed by a flu epidemic. The sadness I saw in Joes eyes, the laughter that was always under his breath, the laughter that could never come out, was because he lost his heart, the day he lost his wife and daughter. I cannot imagine the pain he held inside. Yet, because he had Jesus in his heart, he was able to love me and show me his Jesus. Joes' Jesus.

Life doesn't make sense sometimes. We cannot help the life we are born into, but we can redefine ourselves as we grow older. Our past does not have to become our future. Andrew and I get ready for bed and as he holds me close, I fall asleep with peace and a sense of closure. I am excited about the future and all that my Jesus has planned for me.

I have finally found a place to close my eyes.

Author's Note

My journey to forgiveness was just that....a journey. It was personal and life changing. The ability to forgive those who had hurt, betrayed, and abandoned me seemed impossible. So how did I do it? Let me take you on my journey.

I was a complete mess when I accepted Jesus as my Savior. I had been married many times, and was looking at another divorce. I saw myself as a loser in every area of life. I was hard on myself. I would look in the mirror, and see someone who was unlovable, and someone who didn't know how to love other people. I saw myself as ugly and strange. I didn't trust people; after all they always had a motive for wanting to be around me. I sabotaged every good thing that came my way because I didn't feel worthy to have good in my life and I did not trust that it would even last, so I always quickened the inevitable. In other words, I destroyed everything good in my life before it could be taken away.

The day I accepted Jesus as my Savior, the hole in my heart was instantly filled with His love. But, could I trust Jesus not to take back His love? After all I was the unlovable one, right? I was the strange one and the peculiar one. I stood before my Jesus, and confessed all the dirty little secrets in my life....the shame, the condemnation, the humiliation of all my failures, and the bitterness that had consumed my life. I laid raw, exposed and broken before Him, and on that day my Jesus's love was undeniable. His love comforted me, held me, restored me, and washed me clean.

I had a hunger to know who my Jesus was. I opened His Word and began to devour it. He led me to scriptures like this one in Hebrews 13:5, "I WILL NEVER under any circumstances, desert you (Rachel)nor give you (Rachel) up nor leave you (Rachel) without support, nor will I in any degree LEAVE you (Rachel) HELPLESS, nor will I FORSAKE or let you (Rachel)down or relax MY HOLD on YOU (Rachel), assuredly not." My Jesus will not leave me. There were many scriptures like Deuteronomy 31:8 and Isaiah 41:10 that reassured me that my Jesus was always with me. I took it by faith the same way I learned to take His love by faith.

Just as His Word showed me that He would never leave me, His Word also showed me He did indeed love ME so much that He died for me. I take that personally. When I would read scriptures like John 3:16, "For God so loved the world (I would insert my name here, For God so loved Rachel) that he gave his only begotten Son, that whosoever (Rachel) believes in Him should not perish, but have everlasting life." I still insert my name into scriptures. Why? Because when I read my Jesus's Words, He is talking to me. It is a personal relationship. He is shaping me into how HE sees me.

You may be wondering, what does any of this have to do with forgiveness? Let me continue to take you on my journey.

I had to know that I could trust Jesus to never leave me, and that I was loved by Him. Because of my childhood, this did not come easy. I had to renew my mind in the scriptures Jesus had led me to. It was a spiritual battle in my mind.

The liar would whisper in my ear, "Jesus sees who you really are. Remember your past."

When the fear of Jesus abandoning me would rise, He would bring into mind, the scriptures I had planted in my heart, "I WILL never leave you (Rachel) nor forsake you (Rachel), NO NEVER."

BUT the liar did manage to sow a seed of doubt about my past. How did I know for sure Jesus wouldn't constantly remind me of my past, like so many people had done? Again, He led me to His Word in 2 Corinthians 5:17; Therefore if anyone (Rachel) is in Christ [that is, grafted in, joined to Him by faith in Him as Savior], he (Rachel) is a new creature [reborn and renewed by the Holy Spirit]; the old things [the previous moral and spiritual condition] have passed away.

Behold, new things have come [because spiritual awakening brings a new life]. The minute I received my Jesus as Savior, He saw me as a new creature. I was made new! But I think one of my favorite scriptures is in Isaiah 43:25;"I, only I, am He who wipes out your (Rachel's) transgressions for My own sake, and I will not remember your sins." My Jesus sees me new, sinless, perfect in Him, and He LOVES me!

It was through the Word of God, that I realized I had unforgiveness in my heart toward those who had hurt me. Unforgiveness is like a cancer that will invade every fiber of your being; it will overtake you with bitterness and anger, steal your joy and hinder the calling God has for your life. I used to look at life through the lens of unforgiveness, and it wasn't a pretty lens to look through. I felt justified not to forgive them. I mean, seriously who could blame me, right?

The day I felt God impress into my heart to take care of my dying Mom, I nearly choked on my coffee. It came out of nowhere or so it seemed. I had gotten the news about her cancer and decided I would stay home and wait for her results to come back. We were not only separated by over a 1,000 miles, but by years of no communication, and no relationship.

But God whispered, "Go to her."

"How can I do that? She doesn't even like me. NO WAY! I am not doing it." I yelled back.

"I will help you." God whispered back.

I had a choice that day....to obey God or live a life of unforgiveness. I chose to obey. It was through the obedience of taking care of my Mom that God showed me how to trust Him, obey Him, believe Him, and how to forgive those who had hurt and betrayed me. The 2 ½ year journey of taking care of my Mom and allowing God to show me through His Word how to forgive as He has forgiven me, gave me the freedom to love unconditionally those who had hurt me.

I forever will be thankful that my Daddy God loved me so much, He gave me my Jesus, forgave all my sins, and He didn't leave me to see the world through the lens of unforgiveness.
Even harder, I have forgiven myself, also.

The mind battle is real though, the devil, the great deceiver and liar, always wants to come back, and tries to plant the seeds of doubt, condemnation, humiliation and fear in my mind. BUT, I remind him of what is written in James 4:7 and I have typed it out the way I say it to him:

"So, I have summited to the authority of God. I resist you devil, and I WILL stand firm against you, and you WILL flee from me!"

I have prayed over this book and for everyone who reads it. I pray you will forgive. Never hold on to unforgiveness; it is the devils stronghold and he intends to destroy your life with it. In parting I will leave you with this:

Daddy God, You are the great comforter. I pray for those who do not know You, that they will come to know you, and receive Jesus as their Savior. I pray for the ones who have unforgiveness in their heart, that at this very moment they will surrender it to You and trust You to show them out of the wilderness and bondage and into their freedom, just like you did for me. Thank You, that when life seems impossible, You always show me that with You ALL THINGS ARE POSSIBLE! Amen.

If you need prayer please email me;
rachelsheltonministries@gmail.com
Follow me on Facebook: Rachel Shelton Ministries
& Instagram: @RachelSheltonMinistries

Proceeds from this book support Rachel Shelton Ministries

Made in the USA
Columbia, SC
05 August 2020